MW01634310

CONTENTS

COVER SYMBOL

This diagram was given psychically to M.B.Cooke for the cover of this book. It represents the great pilgrimage which each human soul must make through the cycles of incarnation from darkness into the light. The coils symbolize the long round of death and rebirth. The barbed tail, striking into the heart of the figure, shows that negative and destructive ways only harm oneself, and that in the end evil is its own destroyer. Yet from the very place where darkness dwells can the soul rise up triumphant into the light of its own spirituality, symbolized here by the budding lotus head surrounded by a beautiful auric glow.

Introduction
by M.B. Cooke

The first part of the text following this introduction was transmitted through me telepathically from the source Hilarion in the early part of 1978. The second part was done during 1983. The transmission process I used was the same as for the other books in the Hilarian series, in which a technique of mental or "Raja" yoga is employed to clear the mind of all self-generated thoughts, and to increase the vibration of a contact point at the center of the head. Thought-impressions can then be received and copied down.

The purpose of this introduction is to explain to the general reader, in a non-mathematical way, enough of the fundamentals of astrology to permit him to appreciate fully the material which this book contains.

I mention the *general* reader deliberately because this text, unlike many others on the science of the stars, is *intended* to be read broadly, and not just by students of astrology. Hilarion, the source of this material, wished to provide an overview of the kind of information which the horoscope yields, so that non-specialized readers could understand the way in which the subject of astrology fits into man's great spiritual pilgrimage, and could grasp the nature of the light that astrology can bring to bear upon the complex interplay of karma, rebirth and lesson-learning that affects each life-pattern.

Many readers of the Hilarion series of books have expressed an interest in learning more about the subject of astrology as seen from the higher perspective which he represents. I have offered this material for publication in the hope that through it, these readers and others may discover for themselves deeper insights into the purposes and patterns of life in general.

In my view, it is time for the subject of astrology to come out of the closet and to show us clearly the part it plays in the spiritual evolution of the race. For too long, astrology has been the focus of bitter antagonism between its foes and its partisans, the former blinded by their skepticism regarding all things that are not part of the twentieth century scientific tradition, the latter often equally blinded by their emotional commitment and defensive stance. At times, astrology has been made into a literal religion in which the planets were viewed as omnipotent gods, able to order human lives in a way that did not take into consideration the operation of man's free will, and that ignored totally the many other spiritual considerations that affect the course of man's destiny. One purpose of the Hilarion series of books is to sketch a more broadly encompassing view of the human condition, to bring together the disparate, fragmented disciplines which, like head-strong horses, have for too long pulled away in diverging directions, and to harness them all finally to a single purpose: that of the spiritual advancement of the race.

To this noble enterprise I believe astrology can bring rich gifts, but only when it is approached in a detached way, and with a willingness to learn the *totality* of what it can tell to the race of man, not merely the specific indications for the individual reader.

Thus, although particular information pertaining to individual persons *can* be gleaned from this book, I strongly suggest that it be regarded initially as a general overview and that all parts of it be read. Only after one has grasped the complete pattern of meaning for the different indicators can one really see clearly the way in which these patterns relate to oneself.

So let us turn to the subject of astrology.

As has been explained in Hilarion's other books, astrology is essentially a system of coding by which the guides and guardians of each human soul can "attach" to the new personality projected by that soul, a check-list of traits, tendencies, karmic involvements in the life pattern, most-probable events, and so forth. This is accomplished by timing the birth to coincide with a planetary pattern which the guides have pre-selected as being the most appropriate one.

According to the text following this introduction, these patterns — and specifically the positions of the Sun, Moon and planets in the various signs of the zodiac — are able to either impress certain traits upon the incarnating individual, or represent symbolically the characteristics which the individual has brought with him or will acquire during the life-pattern.

Astrology's raw material consists primarily of the Sun, Moon and planets as seen against the twelve signs of the zodiac. A clear distinction should be made here between planets and stars. Stars are actually bodies like our Sun, but which seem tiny because of their immense distances away from us. By contrast, the planets of astrology are bodies circling our own Sun. The earth is a planet as are Mercury, Venus, Mars, Jupiter, Saturn, Uranus, Neptune and Pluto. Stars shine by their own self-generated light, while the planets are visible because they *reflect* the light from our Sun. The distance of the planets away from us is much less than the distance of even the nearest star. For example, if one could travel at the speed of light (186,000 miles per second), it would take about five hours to reach the most distant planet, Pluto, but over four *years* to arrive at the nearest star. At the same speed, it would take about eight minutes to go from the earth to the Sun.

All of the Sun's planets circle that body in approximately the same plane. For this reason, if we were to observe the motion of any given planet against the night sky for several months or years, we would note that it always stayed close to a particular "path" through the fixed constellations. This path is called the ecliptic in astronomy, and for astrologers it establishes the center of a slightly broader band which encompasses the actual tracks of all the known planets and the Sun and Moon, as seen against the fixed stars. This band is known in astrology as the zodiac.

Astrologers divide this zodiac band or circle into twelve equal parts of 30 degrees each. The marker or beginning point for the division corresponds to the Sun's position in the zodiac band at the beginning of spring.

Luckily, students of astrology do not have to make the laborious observations and calculations that are required in order to know precisely where each planet is located at any given moment. These chores are assumed currently by computers, and the results are generally available in the form of an ephemeris (pl. ephemerides). Most new-age, metaphysical and occult bookstores carry a good selection of ephemerides, usually in the form of books containing tabulations of the positions of the Sun, Moon and planets for each day of a given span of time. The positions are given for either noon Greenwich Mean Time (GMT) for each day, or for zero hour GMT at the beginning of each day. Ephemerides can be readily obtained for all years of the nineteenth and twentieth centuries.

In order to be able to read an ephemeris table, one must learn the shorthand glyphs for the planets and the zodiac signs. These appear in the table below:

THE SUN (Sol)	☉
THE MOON (Luna)	☽
MERCURY	☿
VENUS	♀
MARS	♂
JUPITER	♃
SATURN	♄
URANUS (Herschel)	♅
NEPTUNE	♆
PLUTO	♇

♈	ARIES	Ram	♎	LIBRA	Balance
♉	TAURUS	Bull	♏	SCORPIO	Scorpion
♊	GEMINI	Twins	♐	SAGITTARIUS	Archer
♋	CANCER	Crab	♑	CAPRICORN	Goat
♌	LEO	Lion	♒	AQUARIUS	Water carrier
♍	VIRGO	Virgin	♓	PISCES	Fishes

In an ephemeris, the positions of the various bodies in the individual zodiac signs are given in terms of degrees and minutes into that particular sign. "Minutes" refers to minutes of arc, not of time. Each of the 360 degrees of the circle is divided into 60 minutes of arc, and each minute into 60 seconds or arc. In some ephemerides (Raphael's, for example), the Sun and Moon positions are given accurately to the nearest second of arc, and the remaining bodies to the nearest minute. Below is reproduced part of an ephemeris table for February 1976, showing the way in which the information is usually tabulated.

Day	Sidereal Time (H M S)	☉ Long (° ′ ″)	☉ Decl (° ′)	☽ Long (° ′)	☽ Lat (° ′)	☽ Decl (° ′)
1	8 41 22	11≈15 0	17 S 24	19≈45	5 N 0	10 S 9
2	8 45 19	12 15 56	17 7	2)(9	4 50	6 11
3	8 49 15	13 16 50	16 50	14 21	4 28	2 2
4	8 53 12	14 17 43	16 33	26 22	3 53	2 N 8
5	8 57 8	15 18 34	16 15	8♈15	3 9	6 10
6	9 1 5	16 19 25	15 57	20 3	2 17	9 57
7	9 5 1	17 20 14	15 38	1♉51	1 19	13 21
8	9 8 58	18 21 1	15 20	13 44	0 17	16 14
9	9 12 54	19 21 47	15 1	25 47	0 S 47	18 27
10	9 16 51	20 22 32	14 42	8♊6	1 50	19 52
11	9 20 47	21 23 14	14 22	20 47	2 49	20 19
12	9 24 44	22 23 56	14 3	3♋52	3 41	19 42
13	9 28 41	23 24 36	13 43	17 26	4 23	17 58
14	9 32 37	24 25 14	13 23	1♌27	4 50	15 7
15	9 36 34	25 25 50	13 3	15 53	5 1	11 17
16	9 40 30	26 26 25	12 42	0♍37	4 51	6 43
17	9 44 27	27 26 59	12 22	15 32	4 22	1 41
18	9 48 23	28 27 31	12 1	0≏28	3 35	3 S 28
19	9 52 20	29 28 2	11 40	15 16	2 33	8 22
20	9 56 16	0)(28 32	11 18	29 51	1 23	12 43
21	10 0 13	1 29 0	10 57	14♏8	0 8	16 12
22	10 4 10	2 29 27	10 35	28 6	1 N 6	18 40
23	10 8 6	3 29 53	10 13	11♐45	2 14	19 59
24	10 12 3	4 30 17	9 52	25 6	3 13	20 8
25	10 15 59	5 30 40	9 29	8♑13	4 1	19 10
26	10 19 56	6 31 2	9 7	21 6	4 36	17 15
27	10 23 52	7 31 22	8 45	3≈47	4 56	14 30
28	10 27 49	8 31 41	8 22	16 17	5 2	11 9
29	10 31 45	9 31 57	8 0	28 37	4 54	7 22

Day	♆ Long (° ′)	♅ Long (° ′)	♄ Long (° ′)	♃ Long (° ′)	♂ Long (° ′)	♀ Long (° ′)	☿ Long (° ′)	☊ Long (° ′)
1	13♐27	7♏6	28≏35	19♈8	15♊29	7♑2	23♐55	11 37
2	13 28	7 6	28♏30	19 18	15 37	8 15	23♑35	11 37
3	13 29	7 7	28 25	19 27	15 46	9 29	23 23	11 36
4	13 31	7 7	28 20	19 37	15 55	10 42	23♑20	11 35
5	13 32	7 8	28 16	19 47	16 5	11 56	23 24	11 35
6	13 33	7 8	28 11	19 57	16 16	13 10	23 35	11 34
7	13 34	7 8	28 7	20 7	16 27	14 23	23 53	11 33
8	13 36	7 8	28 2	20 17	16 39	15 37	24 16	11 33
9	13 37	7 9	27 58	20 27	16 51	16 51	24 46	11 31
10	13 38	7 9	27 53	20 37	17 4	18 4	25 20	11 30
11	13 39	7♏9	27 49	20 48	17 17	19 18	25 59	11 29
12	13 40	7 9	27 45	20 58	17 31	20 32	26 42	11 29
13	13 41	7 8	27 41	21 9	17 46	21 45	27 30	11 28
14	13 42	7 8	27 37	21 20	18 1	22 59	28 21	11 27
15	13 43	7 8	27 32	21 31	18 16	24 13	29 15	11 26
16	13 44	7 8	27 28	21 42	18 32	25 27	0≈12	11 25
17	13 45	7 8	27 24	21 53	18 48	26 40	1 12	11 24
18	13 46	7 7	27 21	22 4	19 5	27 54	2 15	11 23
19	13 47	7 7	27 17	22 16	19 22	29 8	3 20	11 22
20	13 48	7 6	27 13	22 27	19 40	0≈22	4 27	11 20
21	13 49	7 6	27 9	22 38	19 58	1 36	5 37	11 19
22	13 50	7 5	27 6	22 50	20 16	2 50	6 48	11 18
23	13 50	7 5	27 2	23 2	20 35	4 4	8 1	11 17
24	13 51	7 4	26 59	23 14	20 54	5 18	9 16	11 15
25	13 52	7 3	26 56	23 25	21 14	6 31	10 33	11 14
26	13 52	7 2	26 52	23 37	21 34	7 45	11 51	11 13
27	13 53	7 2	26 49	23 49	21 54	8 59	13 11	11 11
28	13 54	7 1	26 46	24 1	22 15	10 13	14 32	11 10
29	13 54	7 0	26 43	24 14	22 36	11 27	15 54	11 9

In the far left column, the days of the month appear. Of the remaining columns, only those which have at the top the short form "Long" (longitude) need to be read for the purposes of this book. These columns indicate the zodiac positions of the various bodies. The third column from the left gives the zodiac position for the Sun. The entry for the fifth of the month shows that, at zero hour at the beginning of the day, the Sun was located at 15 degrees, 18 minutes and 34 seconds into the sign Aquarius. Note that the sign appears in the first row of the table but is not repeated until it changes. The column for the Moon's longitude (fifth from the left) illustrates this convention more clearly. At the beginning of the month, the Moon was at 19 degrees, 45 minutes of the sign Aquarius. By the beginning of the 2nd, it had passed into Pisces and had reached 2 degrees, 9 minutes of the latter sign. Therefore the new sign appears. At the beginning of the 3rd, it was still in Pisces, and thus the sign did not have to be repeated.

All of the columns for the planets are read in the same manner. The only additional indicators that should be explained are the two which denote retrograde and direct stations, ℞ and D. For example, in the column for Mercury in the above table, the planet appears, as seen from the earth, to be moving backwards (retrograding) at the beginning of the month. This is evident from the fact that the numbers for the daily positions are decreasing from day to day. However, on the 4th, the letter D indicates that the planet reaches its direct station, after which it moves forwardly (direct motion). Now look at the column for Uranus. This planet has direct motion at the beginning of the month, but on the 11th, it reaches its retrograde station, marked by the letter ℞. After that date, it moves backwards, as seen from the earth (decreasing numbers).

There is but one other area requiring comment, and it is that of aspects. It will be noted throughout the text of this book that Hilarion mentions particular planets being either "in positive aspect to" or "afflicted by" other planets. This is in reference to the number of degrees separating the planets involved in any particular horoscope. When two planets are in a certain degree-relationship to each other (i.e. forming certain angles), they are said to be "in aspect" to each other. The various aspects indicate the extent to which the attributes or qualities signified by the planets involved are able to manifest harmoniously.

For our purposes, there are only five which warrant elaboration:

1) The *conjunction*: two (or more) planets occupying the same degree. This aspect can be either harmonious or difficult, depending on the planets involved. For example, Saturn (cold and restrictive) conjunction Venus (the affections) will tend to limit and chill the love nature. Jupiter (expansion, optimism) conjuncting Venus, on the other hand, will have quite the opposite effect.

2) The *sextile*: two planets separated by 60 degrees (i.e. two signs apart and occupying approximately the same degree within those signs). This aspect is a positive one, indicating that the opportunity exists for an easy merging of the two basic qualities involved.

3) The *square:* two planets separated by 90 degrees, and, as the name implies, a difficult aspect. It indicates two qualities in uneasy struggle with each other, neither permitting the other a full and harmonious manifestation in the life.

4) The *trine*: two planets separated by 120 degrees. This is a most benefic aspect, indicating a harmonious relationship between the planets involved, each planetary quality assisting the positive manifestation of, and contributing to the strength of, the other.

5) The *opposition*: two planets 180 degrees apart, directly opposed to each other. This is a difficult aspect as it involves a relationship between two planets in which one quality can manifest fully only at the expense of (and usually to the detriment of) the other. To balance the two requires conscious and deliberate effort.

Enough has now been given to allow the general reader to follow Hilarion's thesis with relative ease. There is only one point which I would like to emphasize before closing.

It will be clear to the reader from what has been given above, that each individual birth date will find a given planet in only one of the twelve signs. Since Hilarion's text deals separately with each planet in each of the signs, only one-twelfth of the information in this book will apply directly to the reader. And yet, assuming that each of us has lived many times before on the earth, it is reasonable to suppose that we all have had to work through many of the patterns and lessons that are designated by planetary placements other than those which apply to us in this particular life-experience. In light of this, I would underscore again the importance of reading through the entire text before attempting to assess one's own planetary pattern. Once the full text has been perused, the significance of the individual delineations for each planet will become even more meaningful. One will be able to assess the particular points against a much broader backdrop of spiritual understanding.

For readers who have not yet read the other books in the Hilarion series, I recommend that they consider doing so in conjunction with a study of the present work. Many of the discussions in this book will acquire deeper meaning and significance when one has become familiar with the approach to life's purpose as explained in *The Nature of Reality, Seasons of the Spirit* and *Symbols.*

Maurice B. Cooke
Toronto, Canada
January, 1980

A glossary of astrological terms used in this book
is included at the back, for the benefit of readers
who have not made a detailed study of this subject.

The Planets
in the
Signs

Introduction
(Hilarion)

The subject of Astrology is one which is very poorly understood by mankind at the present time. It is thought to be a system by which the meaning of life's events can be understood. It is thought to be a program for the life in terms of timing and patterns which take place during the course of a lifetime. It is thought to be a symbolic description of the inner workings of the mind, the psyche and the personality. But none of these concepts goes to the heart of the astrological system.

In the distant past, when man was making his first appearance on the surface of the earth, the skies did not appear as the now do. The planets were different and had different orbits and periods. There was not the same form of correlation between planetary movements and events upon the earth that there now is. Indeed, very little of significance could have been read in the paths of the planetary bodies, even had man been intelligent or educated enough to discern the movements and geometry of the planets of the solar system.

But when the reincarnational arrangement was initiated, after the inter-breeding of men and angels about five million years ago, it was felt that the best way to teach man about himself and about the spiritual pilgrimage upon which he had embarked, was to cause the planetary bodies to reflect exactly the times and the spirit of the times through which he was living. In addition, it was decided to arrange the birth of each human being to coincide with a geometric pattern of planets which could be read by one properly instructed in order to derive some information about the nature of the incarnating soul, the likely development of the personality, and the most probable series of life-events that would take place.

Yet there is something far deeper to Astrology than these relatively straight-forward facts. It is this: that the astrological system is a direct gift from the highest Creator to mankind. It is a gift which allows him to develop at all levels simultaneously — not only at the physical level where the personality is manifest, but also at the higher mental and astral planes, and those beyond. For it is not sufficient to improve the personality only. There must be an absorption of the improvement at the higher soul level, or what has been termed the higher self.

The planetary energies alone are capable of penetrating through the human being to his higher levels. Without the planetary positions and geometries, as the planets form various angles against the different signs of the zodiac, there would not be the easy communication of lessons and improvements upwardly through the various levels of man's vehicles to the highest point.

It is the purpose of this book to set out in simplified form the meanings of the planets and other astrological symbols, not only for the lower mundane level of the personality, but for the higher self or soul as well. This has never been revealed to mankind hitherto. But time has turned again to a new Age. The cycle of Aquarius is about to begin, and man is at last ready to understand truths additional to those he has already been given.

The Sun

The Sun in astrology denotes characteristics which are a predominant feature of the soul or higher self which has projected the conscious personality. As such, the usual meanings ascribed to the Sun-sign positions must be understood as characteristics which *may* or *may not* be directly and consciously manifested at the personality level, i.e. by the lower self. In many cases, the personality is projected through a complex of hereditary and environmental filters which obscure from the conscious personality some or even most of the Sun-sign characteristics. In such cases, it may always be assumed that one of the tasks of the personality in the incarnation is to find again the obscured features or characteristics and manifest them. There are positive and negative sides to each of the Sun-sign complexes. For example, the positive side of the Aries pattern relates to the abundance of energy which is present, while the negative side is the tendency to allow this energy to express in aggressive or violent behaviour. Similar explanations will be given more fully below for all of the Sun-sign positions. Hence, the task of the personality in which the Sun-sign traits are obscured or repressed is not only to rediscover these traits, but to learn to emphasize only the positive and constructive side.

Aries   We have said that Aries has an abundance of energy available to it. This energy is, in effect, a kind of reward or gift to the Aries individual resulting from acts of courage in past incarnations, when thoughts of self-interest were set aside in order to come to the aid of another. In a sense, the gift is internal rather than external because the very act of courageously facing danger in order to help another person automatically taps deeply into an inexhaustible source of energy, and the soul gains a permanent link with this source of energy. But with every gift comes a responsibility. In the case of Aries, the responsibility is to learn to handle this increased energy so that it does not harm others or the self through aggressive expression and violent behaviour.

Taurus   The Taurus individual has, at the soul level, a deep understanding of the meaning of love. This is attested to by the rulership of Venus over this sign. The grasp of the right approach to love and its true meaning is again a kind of gift which the soul has given itself — in this case, as a result of an incarnation in which a self-sacrificing love was cherished for another, usually without being fully returned. This act of selfless devotion allows the soul to tap deeply into a wellspring of pure love at a very high spiritual plane, which constantly feeds into the soul a great capacity for love and affection. Again, along with the gift comes a responsibility. In the case of Taurus, the task is to learn to express the love side unconditionally, simply allowing the affection to flow into and through the personality without damming it up, and without attaching conditions to the giving of affection. If there is any damming up or restriction of the affectional impulses, a problem arises due to the desire of this abundance of love to find a suitable object. Denied an external abject, i.e. another person or persons, the love will usually lavish itself upon the individual's own physical body with its senses the primary focus. It is from this process that the oft-quoted tendency for self-indulgence in the Taurus stems. Another difficulty can also arise if the nature of suppressive habits in the Taurus individual are such as to prevent the thwarted affectional urges from expressing through self-indulgence. In such instances, it is possible for the love to center not on another individual but on possessions or money. This can occur when in the early childhood there was little physical affection shown by the parents. Thus, in the case of Taurus, the task at the personality level is to express love, without allowing the affectional urges to manifest as self-indulgence or an over-stressing of money or possessions.

Gemini   The Gemini individual is one who, in a past incarnation, developed the intellectual and rational faculties to a marked degree through effort and perseverence, and who used the acquired talents in the service of his brothers. The result of this effort and service is again a gift, in this case a deep tap into the source of intellectual or mind energy at a very high level. This mind energy becomes available to the soul and thus can be manifested in the personality, filters permitting. But again, along with the gift comes a responsibility. In the case of Gemini, it is to learn to manifest the mind energy in a way which does not allow the energy to become dissipated and scattered, and which is not turned against others in the form of verbal attacks. Gemini, with its rulership by Mercury, is often compared to the child phase of human development. Many Gemini individuals remain to some extent at an immature level in terms of the mind energies which they possess. It is commonly observed that children, regardless of Sun-sign, tend to be scattered in their activities, with short attention spans and a difficulty in applying themselves to any long term task with perseverence. This is due to the inability of the immature brain to get into phase with the higher mind impulses. It is also observed that children, particularly when having to live with siblings, develop habits of verbal abuse against each other — often as an alternative form of conflict because the parents inhibit them from actual physical combat. In other Sun-signs where the mind energies are not so strongly present, a point is usually reached where these tendencies are overcome. But in the Gemini, there is so much mental energy that it is much harder, even in maturity, to conquer these negative expressions of the Gemini pattern. Those who fail are found to be either verbally abusive or scattered in their energies, or both.

Cancer   The Cancer individual is one who, in a former incarnation, lived a life of devotion to the family unit, who nurtured and cared for others with great dedication, even though this service might not have been motivated by affection alone. Regardless of motive, the very act of serving the race in this way brings about, at the soul level, a deep tap into a very high source of nurturing impulses, and these are then available to be expressed at the personality level, filters permitting. But with the gift again comes a task: in this case, to express the nurturing instincts without binding others too closely to the self. It is very difficult to expend great energies upon the care and nurture of other souls without allowing some feeling that these other souls "owe something" to the person doing the caring, because of the great sacrifice that is made. But this is the major lesson for the Cancer individual, to care for others without producing guilt in the others and without close-binding those being cared for.

When an individual expends most of his energy in the nurture of others, there is a tendency to feel that without these others remaining in contact, there will be little substance or meaning left to life. The threat of losing the others (for example, when children grow up and leave the home), can be expanded into a general feeling of great insecurity on the part of the Cancer individual, for which the only antidote is trust in Providence or God. When several lives are lived in the Cancerian pattern, the feeling of insecurity can become a trait in the soul which requires correction through an incarnational pattern in which events are arranged to increase the feeling of insecurity in the hopes that the individual will ultimately turn to an inner faith in something beyond man. Usually such a life is preceded by a sequestered life in association with a church or religious organization (monk or nun, for example) in order to give the individual some basis for "remembering" the confidence that faith inspires, when the time of increased insecurity comes.

Leo   The Leo individual is one who, in a past incarnation, showed the trait of leadership and guidance for those who without such help would have perished. From this action comes another gift: in this case, a tap into a spiritual source of initiative and leadership qualities which is always available to the soul, and can be manifested in the personality, filters permitting. But the task which comes with the gift is to express the guidance and leadership without allowing the self to assume too great an importance. These energies are easily misdirected into aggrandizement and pride of self, and constant effort is called for by the Leo personality to avoid these negative traits. The best way to keep the pride and self-centered tendencies from manifesting is to cultivate kindness and consideration for others. But even the kind ones can become enmeshed in a habitual tendency to view life as a kind of play in which they are the principal actor around whom everything revolves. This tendency is again due to the abundance of the energy which is being tapped at the higher level, which comes down as a clear picture of the individual leading others, i.e. at the head of, or in some way above the mass of those who are being led. The best way to deal with the Leo energy is to find an outlet where others are being served at the same time as they are being led or directed. This is why a teaching role is one of the best ways to manifest the Leo nature.

Virgo   The Virgo individual is one who, in a past incarnation, was at an early stage in the learning of certain important soul- or life-lessons. Because of the urgency for every soul to understand all of the basic lessons which the earth was meant to teach, a life in which little is accomplished can justify a special "gift" which is not earned in the same sense as those already discussed. The gift is essentially the loan of certain helpful characteristics from other souls or entities, for the duration of the Virgo incarnation. The mechanism of this loan is too complex to be dealt with here, but it can be taken that at least some of the traits typically expressed by the Virgo individual are not a natural part of the soul. These traits are related to the mental side of the individual. Virgo is an earth sign, which represents the early stage of the learning process. By giving a mental cast to the experience in the incarnation, symbolized by the rulership of Mercury, it is hoped that the individual will be able to comprehend with the rational intellect the lessons which he has not fully grasped with the heart. Then, additional lives can be lived with the purpose of transferring the understanding from the mind to the heart. When the lessons are comprehended by the heart, they are automatically incorporated into the soul at the higher level.

Another superimposed characteristic relates to a set of very high standards of activity, conduct and ideals, which are intended for use as an internal measure of the Virgo's progress, against which he can assess the way his learning is progressing. Where the Virgo consistently falls short of meeting these standards, it can happen that the Virgo begins to apply them to others rather than to the self so as to avoid the chagrin of facing up to failure. When this happens, the critical side of the Virgo comes to the fore. Instead of criticizing himself and correcting the shortcomings, the Virgo turns the scrutiny of his critical eye upon others, and by picking at them verbally attempts to get *them* to conform to the idealistic standards that have been built into *him*.

Libra   The Libran is one who, in a past incarnation, dedicated himself to making a marriage or pair-bond relationship work despite extreme tests and obstacles. Through that effort, the other person in the relationship gained much in terms of understanding about the meaning of personal commitment to and love for another. As a reward for this life of dedication to the ideal of marriage and loyalty, the Libran is given a deep tap into a high spiritual source of intuitive understanding regarding the matter of the one-to-one, committed, dedicated pair-bond. As this intuitive grasp filters down into the lower self or personality, it produces a deep longing for a mate through whom these urges can be fulfilled. But with the gift, again comes a responsibility. There is a tendency at the earth plane level for marriage to be considered as, ideally, the perfect union of two who are exactly suited to each other, who will live happily ever after, etc. This concept, from mythology and folk stories, does not refer to actual workaday relationships between two people, but rather to a deeply obscure *internal* reconciling of opposed polarities within a single individual: the male-female sides, the positive-negative, the dominating-nurturing, etc. Most people come, with maturity, to realize that a working marriage requires compromise, tolerance for the foibles of the other, forgiveness and respect for differences. But for the Libran, with his deep intuitive feeling for the perfectibility of the pair-bond, it is hard to accept that the perfect match is virtually impossible on the earth plane. This is the major lesson for the Libran. It is not one of action or attitude, but rather of understanding at a deep level. There is, however, one primary fault which Librans tend to manifest in their dealings with others, and that is the tendency to be too cold and restrained in their emotional responses. This trait stems from a desire to avoid extremes of any kind, extremes being regarded as threats to the equilibrium of the individual, which at a very deep level are seen as jeopardinzing the chances to achieve that perfect union which the Libran seeks.

Scorpio   The Scorpio individual is one who, in a previous life, killed himself as an act of atonement for some act which he regarded afterwards as being so horrible and detestable as to unfit him to continue living. As a result of this self-destructive act, certain of the darker kinds of energies were tapped into by the soul, which on the one hand give to the Scorpio a deep grasp of the meaning of regeneration through sacrifice and death, but on the other hand lend certain qualities of power over others, a win-at-any-cost attitude, little patience with ideals of fair play and honor, and in his darker moments, a mocking echo of the self-destructive urges that fuelled the original act in the previous life. The great task and challenge for the Scorpio is to manifest the regenerative side of his nature, to rise above the lower self on the wings of an eagle (the higher animal symbol of Scorpio), and to show to others by his own life, the true meaning of the myth of the Phoenix, rising purified from its own ashes. Few Scorpios succeed fully at this task, especially in the past Piscean Age, when few solid guideposts were available to the seeker after spiritual understanding, and chaos and destruction were seen on every hand. But in the new age of Aquarius, it will be largely the Scorpio side of individuals (whether Sun-sign Scorpios or not) which will be in evidence. As the understanding of man opens up to the energies of the new age, his spirit will literally take wing and soar to unimaginable heights of wisdom, love and creative power.

Sagittarius   The Sagittarian is one who, in a past experience, lived a life of honor, integrity and uprightness and who showed to others these qualities in so consistent a fashion that the others were positively helped in their spiritual progress by the experience. The result of the life of honor is a tap into the highest possible spiritual source of such urges, so that they are always readily available to the soul and also to the personality, filters permitting. The task of the Sagittarian is to utilize the urges and to demonstrate uprightness again in this life without allowing the excessive emphasis on honesty and candor to hurt others. It can happen that the Sagittarian is so determined not to hide anything that he fails to consider his thoughts before he gives utterance to them. Not pausing to think of what effect one's words might have on another can lead to embarrassment, awkwardness, and even pain — even though the inflicting of discomfort or pain on another was the farthest thing from the Sagittarian's mind. The major lesson then is not to blurt out thoughts without thinking first what effect they might have on another.

Capricorn   The Capricorn is one who, in a previous life, accomplished much personal success in the world's eyes, but who did so in such a way as to permanently benefit others in a *material* way. Because this does represent a contribution, even though not really at the spiritual level, a tap is permitted into a source of constructive and creative energy which drives the Capricorn to accomplish something worthwhile upon the earth plane. But because the help for others was limited to the material plane, a blindness is introduced into the make-up of the Capricornian personality which makes it more difficult than usual to perceive the reality and value of spiritual concepts and the higher wisdom. Though difficult, it is not impossible, and the Capricornian who succeeds in making of his life a dedication to a higher reality achieves far more and conquers a much greater obstacle than most other souls have to contend with. The goal of a "life of dedication" is symbolized by the Capricornian rulership of the knees, for the knees are the support of the body in the traditional attitude of prayer.

Aquarius   The Aquarian is one who, in a prior life, dedicated his energies to bringing others together into a united group and encouraging love and brotherhood between them. Because the peacemaker is to be honored above all others in spiritual terms, the Aquarian is allowed a special tap into a source of the highest idealism regarding the brotherhood of man, both at the soul level and at the personality level, filters permitting. But this source of ideal brotherhood represents a level of advancement far beyond the achievements of the race to the present day. Love is not universally felt for all; indeed, the only circumstance in which most individuals get even a glimpse of love in its true majesty is that first overwhelming excitement of the love affair, before the cold realities show themselves. But the Aquarian knows instinctively that the universal non-exclusive love is possible, and this often introduces a problem in relating to others at the level which mankind has reached. The Aquarian tends often to seek to approach the ideal he holds within him, and this can lead to a shoving away of the exclusive closeness that marriage implies or a tendency to try to include too many within the circle of aquaintances or friends. The partner then thinks the Aquarian is cold, while the friends can conclude that the Aquarian is too strung-out in his associations. The lesson for the Aquarian is to try to live in the world as it is, and to compromise the ideal brotherhood concept for the sake of becoming close to at least one or two other individuals. Brotherhood starts with two shaking hands. The Aquarian ideal must be nurtured first in groups of small numbers (even two) before the expansion to include the race can take place.

Pisces The Piscean is one who, in a previous existence, ended the life in an act of desperation for no better reason than to end the pain. Suicide is never really justified in spiritual terms, but the least justifiable of all is to take one's own life for motives relating only to the self. Because of this self-destructive act, the Piscean is tapped into a source of despondency and pessimism, which can often filter down to the personality. But it is not the Creator's way to give only the negative. In addition, the Piscean is allowed to tap a deep wellspring of compassion and sympathy for others in the hopes that by occupying himself with the concerns and sadnesses of others, he will forget the melancholy of the self and make of the life a shrine of dedication to others. The sensitivity that results can often drive the Piscean to seek escape from the harshness of life through such avenues as drugs or alcohol. The avoidance of such tendencies is the primary lesson of the Piscean.

The Moon

The Moon in astrology denotes an area quite distinct from those to which the Sun relates. The Moon is the closest of the astrological bodies to the earth, and as such it denotes those influences and characteristics which are acquired on the earth itself, usually in the early portion of the life pattern. It is interesting that although the Moon is a small celestial body, it *appears* as large as the Sun due to its closeness. This is symbolically quite apt, for in the make-up of each incarnated individual, it is common to find that the acquired characteristics loom about as large as those which are inborn and filter down from the soul level. Hence the old argument of psychologists as to which has more importance in the make-up of an individual — the inborn nature or the acquired traits — is perfectly balanced in astrology which declares that in the main, both are of major significance.

The Moon does not act as a filter to block soul-traits from manifesting, nor does it act as an overlay like the other planets, i.e. super-imposing traits that are not present in the soul. It simply reflects to a large degree the "bundle" of characteristics, traits and influences which are seen as likely to be picked up from the environment in the early home conditions. As such, it often will denote some primary trait of a dominant parent, or a general "atmosphere" in the home, such as one of conflict, emotional coldness, etc.

Aries   This sign is ruled by Mars, the planet which governs energy, conflict and emotional explosions. This placement of the Moon always shows that the early home experience was characterized by some lack of control, usually over the combative instincts of those surrounding the child. The result is a stormy early life atmosphere and the risk that the individual has picked up from that experience an unconscious view that "home" means strife and storm. As a result, he may either seek a partner who will cause similar home conditions to be re-created or, once married, may himself try to provoke the kind of storminess which he equates with the concept of home. In every case of the Moon in Aries, it may be said with confidence that an important test for the soul is to overcome the subliminal influence of the early home's strife or conflict, and to refuse to allow it to manifest through him in his own later home experience.

Taurus   This sign is ruled by Venus, the planet of love, affection and beauty. It also rules self-indulgence and the overvaluing of the goods of the world. In the case of this Moon placement, it must be carefully determined whether the Moon is primarily afflicted or well-aspected by other important points in the chart before it can be said which of these two sides has manifested in the early life pattern. Where the Moon is mainly afflicted, it can be assumed that the love atmosphere of the early home was to a large extent curtailed and that as a result it will take more than the usual amount of time to pass before the individual finds an emotionally satisfying relationship in his mature years. The concept of "delayed affectional fulfillment" is thus not an externally imposed condition in the life, but is rather something which arises from the inadequate grasp which the individual has internally upon the notion of what a true love relationship should be. If the Moon is relatively free of affliction, it may be assumed that a generous serving of love was handed out to him in the early home, from one or both parents, and that as a result, his feeling of self-worth and his ability to give and receive love are well-developed (assuming other planetary placements do not contradict).

Gemini   This sign is ruled by Mercury, the planet of the rational mind. The Moon in this segment will always show that the early home influence, as perceived by the child, was one of mental stimulation and an emphasis on achievements of the thinking or rational faculty. There is also a strong suggestion that something pertaining to heightened nervousness or skitterishness was present in the early home environment. Finally, it is likely that something doubled or duplicated was a part of the early home. When the Moon is afflicted in Gemini, it can be assumed that the circumstances of the home were such as to give rise to nervousness or a "nervous disposition" in the individual, or to accentuate latent tendencies in this direction. In such a case the pattern may be looked on as a test of the soul's ability to overcome the negative side of the trait of nervousness, to learn to control the jitters and avoid becoming a "bundle of nerves". When the Moon in Gemini is relatively free of affliction, it will point to the positive side of the Gemini nature as manifested in the home environment, which will usually cause the individual to seek a home in his mature years which is enlivened by study, mental stimulation, much chatter and conversation, and so forth. This desire for mental stimulation in the home may also manifest as a more or less regular changing of address, especially since this is also likely to have been a characteristic of his own early home experience.

Cancer   This sign is ruled by the Moon itself and thus much of what the Moon symbolically represents can find manifestation in the early home life of the individual with this placement. The Moon, in its fullest manifestation, shows its best side in a home environment that is loving and nurturing, with much emotional support and the building of a strong feeling of self-worth. Interpersonal bonds are strong, and the environment is one of complete protection of the family circle from the harshness of the outside world. The whole picture is summed up in the idyllic picture of the cosy family seated in the living room around a blazing fire, the pot on for tea, the family dog curled up and dozing by his master's foot, the howl of the winter storm outside serving but to increase still more the warm glow of "belonging" that all members of the family instinctively feel. But this perfect picture is hardly ever realized in reality. With afflictions to the Moon in Cancer, there is the prospect of falling rather short of the ideal.

The worse the afflictions, the greater the pain of *not* achieving the ideal home environment early in life. As a result of any such lack, it is very likely that the individual will develop an excessive insistence on finding the ideal home situation, and of course will be all the more disillusioned when the day-to-day realities and problems crop up. Such a person needs to learn to accept the world as it is, and people as they are, complete with flaws. Indeed, the inability to accept imperfections is itself an imperfection, and the placement of the Moon afflicted in Cancer is a reminder to the individual that work must be done in the area of accepting things as they are, on compromise, and on putting *effort* into making a home work. A final task of the placement of the Moon in Cancer, whether afflicted or not, is to allow others in the home, especially the children, to be themselves and to be free and unencumbered with guilt or emotional bonds to the parent. The tendency to close-bind the children is especially evident in women with the Moon in Cancer and this trait is one which should at all costs be avoided. It curtails the growth and limits the self-expression of those upon whom it falls.

Leo   This sign is ruled by the Sun, and here we have an exception to the general rule that the Moon relates only to characteristics acquired during the early environment.

In Leo, the Moon does show a soul characteristic. It is that of forgiveness, one of the noblest and most beautiful of all the traits of mankind. This is so because in forgiving another, man patterns himself upon God's own way. God never condemns, and no action, thought or emotion stands in guilt before the eyes of the Father. Man is his *own* accuser and judges himself. His karma is that which he creates for himself and does not come down from some hall of judgement as a retribution for sins. When the Moon in Leo is primarily afflicted, it can be taken that the early home influences were such as to interfere with the natural leaning toward forgiveness that is inborn. Perhaps there was an unyielding or grudge-holding parent; or perhaps the conditions were such that when the individual as a child tried to show forgiveness and tolerance, he was taken advantage of, thought to be weak or mocked in some way. These negative experiences are there as a test to see whether the individual will overcome the obstacles and find again the pure fountain of forgiveness that is his birthright.
 When the Moon is afflicted in this sign, there is also another trait that needs to be worked on, and that is the tendency to turn a blind eye toward the flaws of others and to pretend that the flaws are not there. This is a form of self-deception and inevitably leads to a let-down when the feet of clay show up. Far better to retain a clear picture of people as they are with all their shortcomings, and at the same time to understand that all on the earth are flawed, that it is a part of human nature, and that these shortcomings are all the more reason to love one's brother.

Virgo   The sign Virgo is ruled by Mercury, the planet of the rational mind. In Virgo, the Moon shows that the early home situation was characterized by a mental emphasis and probably by one of the parents being something of a fuss-budget or excessively neat. Something relating to an over-emphasis on detail or form was involved, and probably a commensurate inability to see the broader picture.

"Not seeing the forest for the trees" sums it up in a symbol. When the Moon here is afflicted, it may be taken that the child felt a considerable burden of disapproval or criticism from one or both parents. As a result, there would be a tendency to equate home with an atmosphere of fault-finding and nit-picking, at least subconsciously, together with a leaning toward choosing a partner who exemplifies these traits, or a tendency to exhibit them oneself in the context of the home. Since this trait would not be a part of the soul, but merely acquired through exposure to the early home, the main lesson associated with this placement of the Moon is to avoid allowing one's own home situation in mature life becoming marked by carping criticism, fault-finding and the like.

Libra   This sign is ruled by Venus, the planet of harmony, tranquility, balance, love and beauty. The Moon in this sign at birth denotes an early home environment which was characterized by control of emotional excesses, with at least an outward show of tranquility and harmony. Whether the harmony were really there under the surface can be judged from the degree of affliction to the Moon in this position. A heavily afflicted Libran Moon points to a home life which is superficially smooth and tranquil but with a cauldron of unresolved conflict and turmoil beneath the surface. Since children are far more perceptive than most adults realize, it is certain that a child in such a tightly-capped situation will pick up from his early home life a feeling that home and marriage require an absolute control of the conflict urges within, regardless of the cost. Unfortunately, energies not allowed to release naturally will, without exception, ground out in some less healthy manner. On the positive side, an unafflicted Libran Moon generally shows that the two sides of the individual himself — the male and female polarities — are relatively well integrated and balanced, and that it is likely that a truly tranquil and harmonious home can ultimately be achieved by the individual. It usually happens though that a fully satisfactory marital/home state is delayed for this Moon placement, partly for karmic reasons.

Scorpio   This sign is ruled by Mars and Pluto, together taken to be planets of dark and powerful energies, of sudden and gradual change which strikes to the core of one's being, and of sexual intensity. The Moon in this sign refers to a soul-characteristic and is thus another exception to the general rule. The trait is that of allowing the passionate or sexual nature to dominate the emotional side of the affections. In short, the Moon in Scorpio denotes a person whose sexuality determines in some manner where the affections are placed. Because of the dominance of the physical side of the emotional life, it is found that such individuals are relatively unfamiliar with the feeling of pure affectional love which is unmixed with a passionate or physical component. Since many do not realize that the physical passions are really just another face of love or eros, they might think that they have a difficult time feeling love at all. This is not true, since it is merely that the *way* in which the principle of the love union manifests for them is different. But it remains that a love nature too much in the grip of the physical passions represents an imbalance at the soul level — one which requires correction at the earth plane level in order to be rectified higher up. The way in which the trait is moderated is always one that affects the life of the heart adversely. Typically there is heartbreak, loss or loneliness at some point in the life, the primary purpose of which is to get the soul to see how important the purely *emotional* side of love can be, and what a pronounced effect it can have when a loss is felt by the heart alone. The degree of affliction to the Moon in Scorpio will tell of the intensity of these corrective experiences. Rather little of this placement really describes the early home situation. For this information, one must look to the planets which aspect the Moon, planets in Cancer, or planets in the fourth house of the chart. One thing which can be said, however, is that with severe afflictions to the Scorpio Moon, there would have been some experience, event or circumstance in the early home which served to bring up to consciousness the latent sexuality or sexual awareness of the child. This may be a traumatic event or, on the other hand it may merely be a general attitude of sexual awareness in the home. Karmic patterns determine the nature of this influence.

Sagittarius   This sign is ruled by Jupiter, and when the Moon is placed here, it is certain that something characterized by largeness, increase, joviality, exaggeration, travel or religion (all Jupiter key-words) had some presence in the early home environment. Under affliction, the Moon in Sagittarius shows usually an exaggerated side of the home environment. This could be the importance of the home itself, or too many people involved with the home. When the Moon here is unafflicted, it is likely that the home contributed much to whatever the individual may have in the way of a solid basis for his life, the prosperity which he may enjoy, or the positive quality of his outlook.

Capricorn   Capricorn is ruled by Saturn, the planet of limitation, duty, illness and restriction. The Moon in this sign shows, regardless of aspects to other planets, that the early home experience was characterized by a sense of restriction and limitation. It may have been an emotional coldness or distance which pervaded the early experience, or again, it could have entailed the absence of one of the parent figures. Possibly the early assumption of responsibilities and duties gave to the child his serious and sometimes melancholic view of life. In the home there would have been little laughter, and the adult would look back upon his early years somewhat the way many of the Dickens characters do, as full of hard burdens and unlighted by any gleam of love or lightness. The great test for the Moon in Capricorn is to rise above the dismal home-model he was shown in his own early experience and create a loving hearth where burdens can be set aside and the heart uplifted. It is perhaps too much to expect joy and laughter to ring constantly through the home of the Moon in Capricorn, since these people as children rarely really learn to laugh, but even this can be achieved if enough effort is expended.

Aquarius   This sign is ruled by Uranus, the planet of brotherhood and universal love, but also the planet of unexpected change, rupture and the unusual. The Moon in this sign at birth shows that the early home was touched by the combination of individual encouragement toward freedom and self-expression, together with some down-playing of the emotional or love responses of those in the home. The more afflicted the Moon, the more one will find a sense of emotional control and suppression, even coldness, at the heart level. The more positively aspected the Moon in this sign, the more the positive aspects of encouragement of individuality and independent thinking will be found. Regardless of the aspects to the Moon in Aquarius, there tends to be taken from the early home situation a trait of self-control at the emotional level, a dislike of emotional display or extremes, which can produce a difficulty in the individual's own later home/marriage pattern, particularly if he becomes involved, as he usually does, with someone who requires more in the way of emotional responsiveness than the Aquarian Moon is prepared to give. The test here is to realize that true affectional interchange is *not* contrary to the preservation of individuality and independence. The nature of true and unselfish love has always been to want the fullest flowering of all facets of the other person, without any thought of constraint or limitation.

Pisces   This sign is ruled by Neptune, the god of the sea and ruler of all that is illusory, over-emotional, feeling-oriented and escapist. When the Moon is here at birth, it is inevitable that something about the early home experience is characterized by one or more of these key-words. The possibilities are rather varied, however, and a list would serve no purpose. Regardless of just how the early home reflected the essential nature of the Pisces/Neptune combination, one can safely assume that the individual who lived through it was deeply marked by the experience.

There will be a tendency to expect the later adult home which he creates to reflect the prominent characteristics of the earlier one. This expectation is almost always unconscious (Neptune being the ruler of that which eludes the conscious mind), and therefore it can be expected that if difficulties arise due to these expectations, the individual himself will have extreme difficulty in perceiving that he might be at fault. This is a difficult test to undergo, but the stakes are high and every effort should be made to succeed. If the individual does not perceive the truth about himself in relation to his home/marriage, then he will fail to develop that depth of bond with the other person which is necessary to the continuance of the relationship, and both home and marriage will founder on the rocks of reality.

The Ascendant

The Ascendant is not fully understood by students of the occult at the present time. It is thought to be determined strictly by the timing of the "first breath" of the individual at birth. However, there are complications which can arise in the birth sequence and which can delay or advance the first breath beyond or short of the "best" time in terms of the pattern of life-events, the internal and acquired traits, and so on. Prior to each birth, the days and weeks around the expected end of the pregnancy are scoured for appropriate planetary patterns which accord with the life about to be initiated. When the best day is determined, the 24-hour span of that day is inspected carefully to arrive at the most appropriate Ascendant – one which will cause the planets to fall into the houses in the most significant way for the soul. Then much effort is expended in attempting to orchestrate the order of the birth events so that the chosen day and Ascendant are those of the first breath. In most cases these efforts are successful within one hour. However there are instances where the first breath differs from the preferred time by up to 12 hours or more. In these cases – usually those where the individual is unlikely during his life to seek the aid of an astrologer – there would seem to be some lack of correspondence of the life to the chart if the same were ever erected and studied. The techniques of rectification could be utilized to determine a better Ascendant than the one arrived at from the birth time, but a better method is to consult the subconscious of the individual, which knows the best Ascendant quite well, and can be tapped through the use of the pendulum.

A further difficulty lies in the fact that there can be more than one appropriate Ascendant. For example, there can be a general Ascendant, yielding a chart which gives a good general picture of many facets of the life. Then there can be a "timing" Ascendant which provides a better idea of the sequence of life events through the application of transits and progressions, etc. There could also be a "karmic" Ascendant yielding a chart which is read only for Saturn aspects to determine the karmic patterns in the life. And there are other appropriate Ascendants as well, but they are more rare.

What we are going to discuss here, however, is the first-breath Ascendant, which tends to act as an extraneous influence that overlays certain traits into the personality, particularly in regard to the *self-image*. The picture one has of oneself is of great importance in any life pattern, for if it is seriously flawed or deficient in some way, much in the way of obstacles and blockage can be present in any attempt to manifest positive characteristics.

Aries   The sign Aries rising will tend, due to its rulership by Mars, to give to the developing self-image a coloring of action and courageousness. The person will see himself as quick to respond to situations, particularly to emergencies, and as being something of a leader or a model for others to emulate. Emotionally there will also be the quick response, finding an extreme in sudden infatuations and the like. An interest in physical activity for its own sake will be present, and probably a continuing interest in sports or athletics. The self-image as the admired athlete is not uncommon, though it may be repressed and not shown to others.

Taurus   This sign when rising will color the self-image with the solid hues of earthiness, practicality and solidity.

There will be the tendency to view oneself as having both feet on the ground, and the traits of consistency and dependability will also be a part of the self-picture. It is to be emphasized that, in reality, none of these traits may be present as viewed by others. The Ascendant shows only the *self-view*, which may differ rather a lot from the picture that other people have of the individual. This is why it is not uncommon for people to recognize themselves more readily in the traits belonging to the *ascending* sign than in the traits of the Sun-sign.

Gemini   This sign when rising will give to the self-image an aspect of mental emphasis, due to its rulership by Mercury. The self is viewed as being quick and alert mentally, as being versatile and creative, and as being something of a conversationalist or a wit. These traits may be imaginary or real, but they certainly will influence the way the individual interacts with others.

Cancer   With Cancer rising, the self-image will be dominated by the picture of the home-maker (especially for women with this sign rising). The image one has of the self is colored by notions of nurturing and protecting others, of providing for them and caring for their needs. This may in many cases actually lead to a seeking out of a life pattern which will allow these traits to manifest, due to the fact that the Moon, which rules Cancer, is such a powerful influence on the developing psyche of an individual. When Cancer rises, it may be taken that the intent of those selecting the birth-chart for the individual was to provide an influence which would introduce into the make-up traits which either are not there through other influences, or if present, are in some way unbalanced or inadequate. The intent then is to help the individual to correct a problem that he has had with the notion of home and the nurturing function.

Leo   When the sign Leo rises, there will be a tenden-- cy for the self-picture to be colored by the notions of elegance, specialness and superiority. A proudness will often be felt internally, even though it usually does not manifest. The reason for giving this Ascendant to an individual is to prompt him to think better of himself than he is in the habit of doing when in incarnation. The rulership by the Sun thus lends to the individual certain bolstering influences in terms of how he sees himself, which are intended to teach him not to underestimate his own worth and not to feel inferior to others. In view of this explanation, it will be understood that those with Leo rising will often find that they are torn between thinking little and thinking a lot of themselves. Through the experience of this inner battle, it is hoped that they will ultimately learn that each person is complete and worthy in his own right, and that none are either superior or inferior.

Virgo   When this sign rises, it tends to color the self-picture with the ideas of neatness and fastidiousness. The self is seen as articulate, organized and in control. There will also be some tendency to see oneself as having high standards of behaviour (whether true or not), and there may be some tendency to apply these standards to others and find them wanting. A critical trait may then surface.

Libra   When Libra is on the Ascendant at the first breath, the self-picture is characterized by the ideas of emotional control, placidity and even temperment. The individual sees himself as not having extremes of feeling or behaviour, and tends to idealize this mode for himself. Alas, the reality is almost always the reverse as seen from outside of the self. For the sign Libra ascending is given usually to insert into the make-up some factor which will prompt an attempt at controlling the energies, emotions, and thoughts, since this has not become a part of the soul in previous incarnations. This is why one will often note, in those with Libra rising, a tendency to oscillate between extremely controlled behaviour and explosions of emotional energy — often leaving others totally perplexed and at a loss to explain the sudden change. The best symbol here is the volcano which for years is inactive and then one day erupts in fury. The sign Libra rising will also color the self-image with the hues of beauty and attractiveness, and very often the person will indeed be very nice to look at. Libra rising will prompt the individual to maintain and improve whatever pleasantness there may be in the appearance.

Scorpio   The sign Scorpio on the Ascendant will, due to its rulership by Mars and Pluto, lend to the self-image the traits of intensity, moodiness and control over others. Again, none of these may actually be present, but the individual will see himself in this light nonetheless. Further, there will be the coloring of a brooding sexuality which often can manifest in dealings with others as a pattern of conquest in the bedroom. The Scorpio Ascendant is given not to add these traits necessarily, but rather to cause the individual to attract into his life, by the natural laws of affinity, certain experiences of a karmic nature which will allow him to set aside a portion of the large karmic burden which he usually brings into incarnation with him.

Sagittarius This sign rising will tend to make the individual see himself as upright, honest and morally strong, whether true or not. It will also give him a yearning to "see the world" through travel. There may even be in the self-picture some aspect of the "Wandering Jew" syndrome. In its effect upon the life, Sagittarius rising often delays marriage or causes there to be more than one marriage-like relationship, usually because of a tendency to cling to the youthfulness and adventurousness of the sign Sagittarius for many years after others have abandoned the excitement of their youthful dreams. This is not by any means to criticize the tendency of retaining a youthful outlook. Indeed, most people in the world now take up far too serious and heavy an attitude to life at an early age, turning their backs on the sense of fun and excitement which the Creator intended man to carry with him all his days.

Capricorn   This sign rising, through its rulership by Saturn, lends all that can be imagined in the way of seriousness to the self-image. There tends to be the idea of "an old head on young shoulders", and the view that "life is hard and life is earnest" is often inculcated into the developing self-picture. Sometimes this is due to experiences with ill-health or early responsibility in the life pattern, which would have been arranged in order to augment the serious side of the inner picture. Inevitably, the sign Capricorn rising at birth is given to counterbalance a general tendency in the soul to lack seriousness, to be too casual in dealings with others. This is why individuals with this sign rising will generally feel torn between a tendency to take things quite lightly and the reverse trait of over-seriousness. The goal is of course to find the balance between them which will allow a middle path to be charted.

Aquarius   When Aquarius rises in the natal chart at first breath, it lends to the self-image certain traits of independence, individuality and intellectual ability. The self is seen as "different" from others, unusual in some way. In most cases of Aquarius rising, the pattern is arranged in order to encourage the individual to "branch out", to strike some new note while in incarnation, to break the old familiar patterns of other lives. Often there has been too much repetition of conventional ways of living, and the soul is "in a rut", as it were. Thus one can expect a certain alternation in the individual between times of conventional behaviour and times of quite unconventional activity as he seeks the balance between the two tendencies.

Pisces   The sign Pisces rising will color the self-image with hues of melancholy and victimization. The person will feel in many ways down-trodden or under the heavy hand of fate. The "sad sack" image attaches to the self-picture and it is extremely hard to make the individual see that life need not be as glum and pessimistic as he makes out. In this case, the rising sign influence is a test: to see if the heaviness can be overcome by positive effort.

The Midheaven

Like the Ascendant, the Midheaven or M.C. (medium coeli) is not fully understood by students of the occult at present. Essentially, the M.C. shows the other part of the self-picture: that which is projected out to the world. In this sense, it is the facade which an individual assumes in order to function effectively among others. Thus the Ascendant and the M.C. show the two halves of the ego or lower self. It should be emphasized however that the influence of the M.C. is not so much one of direct cause and effect, in the scientific sense, as it is with the Ascendant. It is more of an "arranged" influence, i.e. the life pattern is adjusted to develop an outer image reflecting in some manner the sign on the M.C. and the planets in the tenth house.

Aries　　　This sign on the M.C. will show a tendency to appear to others as headstrong, willful and dynamic, whether the internal self-image corresponds or not. There could be a tendency to appear hot-headed, especially if Mars or Uranus were located in the tenth. Conversely, a planet like Saturn in the tenth with Aries on the M.C. would serve to lend a heaviness and a kind of brooding control to the Arien energies, which would nonetheless be apparent to others. Feminine planets in the tenth with Aries on the M.C. will shift the impulsiveness into the affectional sphere.

Taurus　　　Taurus on the M.C. indicates that the outer facade appears to be strongly colored by affectional urges and by the desire to interact emotionally with others.

"Very loving" is an expression others might use to describe the individual, provided there were no counter-indicating planets in the tenth. For example, Saturn there would close down the demonstration of affection, while Mars would tend to promote a lack of consistency and a certain storminess in the affectionate image being projected.

Gemini   With this sign at the M.C. there will be a note of intellectual ability or versatility projected forth to others. The individual may appear something of a wit or a good conversationalist. These traits could be subdued with contrary planets in the tenth, however. Saturn would lend a heaviness or plodding character to the interchanges with others, while Mars would sharpen the tongue and promote altercation and disputes.

Cancer   When Cancer appears on the M.C., the image projected forth to the world is one which contains elements of the nurturing, caring and protective side of the sign. Cancer at the Midheaven is usually accompanied by Libra on the Ascendant, and it will be understood from the previous description of Libra ascending that the combination of these two signs to represent the inner and outer picture respectively will prompt the individual to seek out some form of domestic or home environment (Cancer) so that the lesson of balancing the emotional nature (Libra) can be learned. The over-control of emotional expression which Libra overlays upon the inner picture is at odds with the tendency from previous lives to be *not enough* in control, and since the home environment is conducive to bringing emotional conflict into the open, it makes an excellent arena in which the inner conflict can be waged.

Leo   With Leo at the Midheaven, the image projected
to the world has elements of magnanimity, pridefulness,
generosity and occasionally arrogance. This picture may
not conform to the inner picture and it may not be very
close to the real complex of qualities in the individual, but
it is given primarily to allow him to overcome feelings of
inferiority which are inevitably carried over from a previous existence. In this case, even if the individual has a
shaky inner self-image, the prompting to put a brave face
forward, which Leo at the M.C. gives, may eventually
cause the inferior inner picture to change. This is due to
the great power of *action* in the world, not only in its
effect on the physical level but on the emotional and mental levels as well.

Virgo   This sign at the M.C. gives a tendency to project the characteristics of punctiliousness, practicality and
a sense of the importance of detail and organization. A critical streak may also be observed by others as well as a certain idealistic tendency. In the case of this sign at the Midheaven, it may be taken with confidence that the soul has
at least one extremely important lesson to learn in this life.
The key to the lesson is the position of Saturn in the chart.
By house and/or sign, this planet will designate a learning
area of the utmost importance to the soul. This is not to
say that there would not be additional important lessons as
well.

Libra   Libra at the M.C. will indicate one who habitu-
ally projects an image of refinement, calm and emotional
control. These traits are often not really present in the
make-up of the individual. The intent of placing Libra on
the Midheaven is to prompt the person to increase his control over the emotional nature, much the same as with
Libra rising.

Scorpio   With this sign at the top of the chart, there will be a tendency to project an image of sexuality, although this projection may be entirely unconscious on the part of the individual with this placement. Others will perceive the person as being attuned to the fine nuance of sexual energies present in any gathering of people, and usually the opposite sex will perceive the individual as radiating some indefinable aura of sexual attraction.

Sagittarius   This sign on the M.C. at birth will cause the individual to tend to project an image of uprightness, candor and a youthful, adventurous spirit. Many with Sagittarius at the M.C. have Pisces rising, and in such cases the purpose of the positive and buoyant sign on the Midheaven is to act as a counter-weight to the more melancholy and subdued inner picture which Pisces confers.

Capricorn   This sign appears commonly at the M.C. coinciding with either Aries or Taurus rising. It tends to cause a projection of the more serious and cautious traits of Capricorn into the outer picture. Others will see the individual as practical and hard-working, with little time for play. But play is precisely the right prescription for these individuals, particularly those with Taurus rising. In such cases the preponderance of earth on the angles weighs down the spirit and must be counteracted with light, enjoyable activity undertaken for pleasure alone. Those with Aries rising should also avoid the trap of "all work and no play" which Capricorn at the M.C. sets. In the latter case, sports activities are a more natural outlet than with Taurus rising.

Aquarius   This sign at the M.C. points out a tendency to project a picture of independent thinking, emotional control and a certain "difference" which others will be hard put to define. The primary importance of this sign on the Midheaven is its tendency to cause a covering over of the affectional urges. A crust forms, and it is the task of the soul to learn to express the love nature freely despite this mask of indifference.

Pisces   This sign on the Midheaven tends, in northern latitudes, to coincide with Cancer rising (although Gemini rising will be encountered in a minority of cases). When the two water signs are on these important angles, there is an almost overwhelming tendency to show an emotional face both inwardly and outwardly. This will be accompanied by feelings of insecurity and victimization. The whole picture presents a great obstacle which the soul has freely chosen in order to learn once and for all how to ride herd on the emotional nature. In past lives there would have been too little effort put into control of the emotions, and the present life can be looked on as a "last, best chance" to succeed. It is like learning to swim. If you learn with a bathing suit on, you will likely master the art well enough. But if you purposely attire yourself in rubber boots and three heavy sweaters, then if you can learn to swim despite the extra drag, you will *really* have learned. This is akin to what the soul does in taking on the two water signs at birth.

Mercury

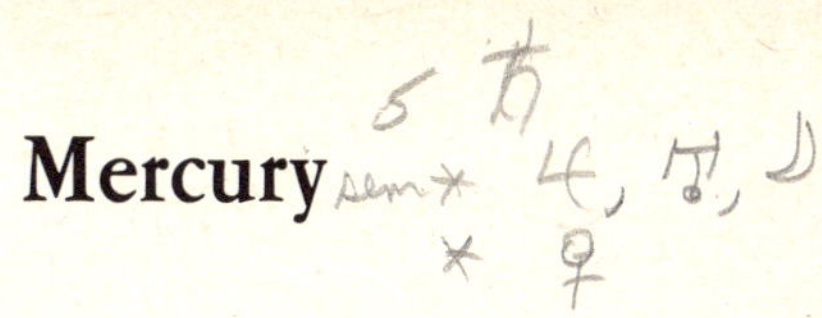

The planet Mercury in astrology is the primary symbol for the mental or rational faculty in man. It is thus one of the three basic symbols for the tripartite nature of man: the mental, the emotional and the physical. Mercury is a planet which acts strictly as an "overlay" to the basic traits and characteristics which are projected down from the higher self or are picked up in the early home environment. If Mercury is in the same sign as the Sun, it will intensify the basic Sun-sign characteristics through its overlay action. If it is in a different sign, it will produce a contrast between the instinctual reasoning process (Sun-sign) and the rational or conscious reasoning process. If Mercury is conjunct or semi-sextile to the Sun within three degrees, it may be assumed that the mental traits shown by the sign holding Mercury are a *part* of the higher self, although Mercury will nonetheless act to intensify these traits through its overlay function. Outside of three degrees orb, no such assumption about the higher self can be made.

The overlay applied by Mercury on the mental aspect of an individual is always arranged for the purpose of allowing him to learn certain basic and important lessons. When Mercury intensifies the Sun-sign traits by being in the Sun-sign, one important lesson will be to overcome any tendency to manifest mainly the negative side of the Sun-sign, or to be less overbalanced or extreme in manifesting the Sun-sign characteristics. When Mercury is in a different sign than the Sun, the basic traits and lessons given hereunder may be assumed.

Aspects   Aspects to Mercury from other planets suggest something of the way the mental overlay of Mercury is likely to manifest. Afflictions will tend to produce the negative side of the sign holding Mercury as these touch upon the mental life, while positive aspects will bring out the positive side of the sign.

In general, aspects to *Saturn* will produce either seriousness or depression depending upon the nature of the aspect.

Uranus will give either flashes of insight or a tendency toward mental breakdown.

Mars produces either great mental energy or mental combativeness (abusive streak).

Neptune gives either vivid imagination (even a visionary quality) or a draining of the mental energies through day-dreams, castles-in-the-air, etc.

Venus positive to Mercury makes the voice pleasant and gives an appreciation of the "mental" arts: music, literature, poetry, etc. Venus negative tends to waste the mental energies on affectional day-dreams, infatuations, etc.

Jupiter positive gives an abundance of all mental qualities, especially those of the signs holding Mercury and Jupiter. Jupiter negative causes something to be greatly exaggerated in the mental make-up.

The *Moon* positive to Mercury brings many different facets of the mental abilities together. The Moon rules the "everyday" mental activities (i.e. those required for driving, walking, doing dishes, etc.). To have the rational side and the everyday side in harmony releases extra energy and ability into the mental sphere. Inharmonious aspects between the Moon and Mercury also dump energy into the mental sphere, but the energy is difficult to handle. It will often be frittered away on endless chatter, gossip, cattiness, etc.

Aries   Here the impulsiveness and need for control will be found in the mental characteristics of the individual.

Considerable mental energy will be present which can be put to good use once the person learns to control the mind, to keep it in a single channel long enough to accomplish something. The basic lesson here is to *achieve mental control*.

Taurus   Mercury here shows, if afflicted, an overlay of self-absorption, the thoughts turning ever to the self. Real shocks will be needed to bring the person to the point of considering others ahead of the self. Such shocks can be expected in the case of Mercury in Taurus badly afflicted, and will occur in the personal affectional life, especially in relation to children (ruled by Mercury). In affliction, Mercury here also renders the throat and neck a weak location, susceptible to illness etc. The basic lesson is to *overcome self-absorption*. In positive aspect, Mercury here shows a love of beauty, especially the mental arts of music, literature, etc. and conveys an ability to verbally express affection in a touching manner.

Gemini   Mercury here if afflicted promotes the essential Gemini failings: scattered forces and using the tongue to hurt others. The basic lesson is to *curb the hurtful tongue*. If positively aspected, Mercury gives versatility, good conversational ability, a gift for expression and sometimes linguistic abilities.

Cancer   Mercury here if afflicted will make it very difficult for the rational mental processes to operate independently of and unaffected by the emotional life. Negative feelings and emotions will have a way of muddying up the reasoning ability. The main lesson is to *separate thought from emotional influences*. If well aspected in Cancer, Mercury gives a love of home and especially, warmth for children within the family circle.

Leo   Mercury here if afflicted will aggravate feelings of pride, superiority and arrogance. The thoughts will revolve ever and only about the self, and the person's life will seem to him to be a magnificent play in which he himself is the main actor, and has written all the parts. The main lesson is to *see others as whole persons in their own right,* living their own life-plays. Again, as with Taurus, shocks are to be expected in order to force the attention away from the self. These will come in relation to love affairs and also to children.

Virgo   Mercury here if afflicted lends the traits of criticism and over-idealism to the mental nature. The main lesson is: *Accept others with all their faults; do not seek to perfect the world until you yourself are without flaws.* Well-aspected, Mercury here gives excellent gifts of mental precision, analytical ability and an inventory-like recall.

Libra   Mercury here if afflicted will give the trait of rigid mental control over shows of emotion. This is its primary effect. The main lesson is to *be more demonstrative with affection.* If well-aspected here, Mercury overlays a tendency to seek a partner at an early stage of life. There is a natural feeling of the "rightness" of the pair-bond.

Scorpio   Mercury here if afflicted brings a tendency to be mentally preoccupied with sexuality to an excessive degree. There is also a tendency to develop an "earthy" or sexy voice. The main lesson is to *think less about sexual matters.* Well-aspected, Mercury here gives an ability to do well financially.

Sagittarius Mercury here if afflicted promotes criticism of others, thus the main lesson is to *curb criticism.* Well-aspected, it gives a distinctly youthful and adventurous outlook on life which persists into old age.

Capricorn   Mercury here if afflicted makes the mind extra serious and "weighed down" by thoughts of future risk, fears, responsibilities, etc. The main lesson is to *fight the over-serious tendency in the mind,* and the best way is to find some source of joy and levity in the life which can be as an antidote to the sober cast of the mental attitudes.

Aquarius   Mercury here is an excellent placement regardless of aspect, as it is exalted in this airy, mental sign. Even in affliction, the worst that Mercury can do is to overlay an excessive degree of mental activity into the nature. The afflicted Aquarian trait of affectional coolness will also be present to some extent, although this is not hard to overcome if no other promoters of emotional over-control are in the chart. Positive aspects to Mercury in Aquarius merely give an abundance of mental and intellectual abilities.

Pisces   This is beyond any doubt the most difficult placement for Mercury, regardless of its aspects. Pisces is the fall of Mercury (opposite which Mercury rules), and every imaginable obstacle to the smooth and efficient functioning of the rational reasoning faculty can be found with this placement: draining away of mental energy (Pisces ruler Neptune saps the substance of anything it touches); emotional states having too much influence on thought or preventing clear thinking; excessive worry; pre-occupation with pessimistic thoughts like death, loss, etc.; dwelling on past sorrows; overactive imagination and day-dreaming; and a host of others. Even with mainly positive aspects some of these negative traits will be found, although the sponge-like retentivity will also likely be present. As the aspects to Mercury in Pisces become more and more difficult, so one will find more and more of the above negative traits manifesting, and to a more and more pronounced degree.

Venus

The planet Venus is the main astrological symbol for the affectional and feeling side of man. It is important to understand that the emotions other than love and affection all stem from the pure essence of the love part of the triangle, but represent perversions, contortions or negations of it. Thus, fear and hate are its opposite, pity and sentimentality are contortions, and lust or any inordinate desire to "possess" another can be thought of as perversions of the love facet.

In astrology, Venus acts as an overlay influence, impressing upon the forming personality certain characteristics pertaining to the affectional sphere which belong to the sign holding Venus. When Venus is within three degrees of an exact aspect to the Sun, it may be assumed that the trait suggested by the placement of Venus is also present at the soul or higher-self level. The following meanings and basic lessons apply:

Aries   Venus afflicted in Aries gives an impetuous streak to the affections and a great difficulty in controlling the love urges. Sudden infatuations are common. The main lesson is to *control the impulses in the area of the affections.* This does not mean to choke out the showing of affection, but rather to make sure of how one feels before leaping into a relationship. Love takes time to grow and flower. It cannot be manifested between two people overnight, with rare exceptions. Even when not badly afflicted, Venus in Aries tends toward impetuousness in love.

Taurus   This sign is ruled by Venus and thus it tends to bring out the best side of the love nature even when the planet is afflicted. In grave affliction, Venus here tends to over-stimulate the love-nature to such an extent that other facets of the life can be by-passed. "All for love and the world well lost" about sums it up. Even this is not such a terrible thing because of the importance of the love-lessons for the human race in the present cycle of incarnation. Well-aspected, Venus here lends to the love nature all that can be desired in the way of constancy, depth of feeling and genuineness of affection.

Gemini   When Venus here is in affliction, there is a tendency to become involved in more that one relationship at a time, not necessarily because these are "arranged", but because the outer circumstance reflects something of a split love-nature inside the individual. There is the capacity to feel two or more different kinds of love or affection equally strongly (the versatility concept of Gemini), and the willingness to try to experience both simultaneously. When this trait manifests, it can be taken as definite that a test is being conducted in the life in question. The test is to see whether the individual can perceive that a truly deep love experience within the context of present-day conditions can only be had by concentrating on one other individual. To the extent that the person with this placement fails to limit himself to a single partner, to the same extent will sorrow and loss come into the life. Events are arranged so that of the two (or more) others being kept "on a string", the one to cut off the relationship first will be the one for whom the greater love was felt. The positive aspects to Venus here lend a certain light flirtatiousness to the nature, and a tendency to be attracted to clever or intelligent people.

Cancer   In this sign of exaggerated feeling, Venus afflicted will cloud the love nature with excess emotionalism and a tendency to lose control of the love impulses when a strong relationship comes along. It is important for people with this placement to try to keep themselves in control of their feelings even while allowing love to manifest. This is a problem which will be understood only by those who have Venus in Cancer (or possibly in Pisces). Well-aspected, Venus here gives a very warm love-nature, and one that seeks to find its best expression within the context of the home environment.

Leo   Venus in this sign afflicted will give great idealism to the love nature, but by the same token can lead to great disappointments when the flaws of the adored person begin to show up. The main lesson is to see, with eyes unclouded by idealistic self-deceptions, that all on the earth have weaknesses and failings, and to love them even with all their flaws.

Virgo   Venus here afflicted gives excessive ideals in regard to the love partner — so much so that few if any seem to measure up. This can lead to long lonely periods in the life, or, where a partner is taken, a trait of endless criticism. The main lesson of the placement is to accept others as they are and to curb the critical nature, especially toward those for whom affection is felt.

Libra   Venus is the ruler of Libra, and even in affliction a deep, sensitive love-nature tends to manifest. Grave afflictions will lead to indecisiveness in choosing a partner, but at worst this will produce a minor delay in affectional fulfillment. Generally, Venus in Libra is an excellent augury of happiness in marriage at some point in life, and it may be taken that this will come as a karmic 'reward' for having sacrificed much in a past life due to a deep and (usually) unrequited love felt for another. Almost always this "other" will be the very soul with whom, in the present life, happiness will eventually be found.

Scorpio   Venus here, whether afflicted or not, is badly placed by sign. Scorpio is the detriment of Venus (opposite a sign it rules), and it is very difficult for the pure love feelings to manifest for anyone with this placement. Instead, the love nature tends to be clouded with physical urges, and the resulting passionate nature can and often does lead to sorrow through loss of the one for whom the affection is felt. The essential lesson here is to realize that love can be complete without having to manifest at the physical level as well. The emotional side of love is an integrated thing and does not need the physical side. This is not to say that the two must be divorced — quite the contrary. When a true love/affection relationship exists for a man and a woman at the purely emotional level, it is natural that it should wish to express through the physical body as well. To deny such an expression will actually damage the emotional side in the long run. The trick is to see that the emotional side of love does not depend on or draw any strength from the physical side.

Sagittarius   Venus here when afflicted shows in the higher self such a love of adventure and travel for its own sake that there is a tendency to by-pass the opportunity for a love relationship in favor of the open road, as it were. In order to show the individual the relative importance of affection, it will always be arranged for the person to carry on a love relationship at long distance, with a considerable period of separation from the affectional partner. In this way it is hoped that the longing for a closer contact will touch the higher self and re-balance the attitudes toward love. Thus this placement, unlike most others for Venus, does show a soul trait which needs correction.

Capricorn   Venus in this sign, when afflicted, tends to dampen the love nature with a certain coldness or distance. This may not be perceived by the individual as much as by others, due to Saturn's (ruler of Capricorn) often subconscious influence. The main lesson is to show affection and warmth more. In positive aspect, Venus in Capricorn is dedicated, long-suffering and constant in the affections.

Aquarius   Venus here when afflicted brings traits of emotional coldness and an inability to show genuine warmth and affection to another. In every case of such a placement, the difficulties in the love-life which this trait causes are karmic for having chilled the affectional warmth which another had felt for this person in a previous life.

Pisces   Venus here if afflicted will, even more than in Cancer, cloud the affectional life with excessive emotionalism and sentimentality. There will be a tendency to abandon oneself to the love instincts without a thought for balance or for permanence. This of course is bound to lead to sorrow and loss in the affectional sphere, and the purpose of such difficult experiences is to encourage the individual to gain some measure of control over his love nature — again not to clamp it off, but rather to express love in a constant manner which is not at the mercy of passing emotional states, fears, etc.

Mars

The planet Mars in astrology represents the energy with which the physical body carries out its various functions: muscular, mental, emotional and procreative. All of these activities require energy to be expressed through the physical and in a deep sense, all of these energies are the same. They are the gift of life, in a sense, for without them life cannot be and cannot renew itself. The gift is directly from the will/power/creativity part of the divine triangle, and is an essential part of all creatures who are "made in the image of the Creator", i.e. who have all three facets of the triangular nature of the divine source.

The placement of Mars in the birth chart of an individual tells something of the nature of the energy to which he has access, and hints at certain lessons that will have to be learned through the struggle to control and channel the energy.

Aries　　　This sign is ruled by Mars and the result of having Mars in its own "home" is an abundance of energy capable of being used in a multitude of ways. It is not limited to physical or muscular energy by any means, but can equally well express itself through procreativity, mental work or emotional experience. When Mars here is afflicted, the over-riding necessity is to *learn to control the energies.* It is difficult for Mars afflicted to control itself, regardless of sign, but in Aries, where it receives an excess, the problem is that much more acute. In positive aspect, the indication is simply that of a super-abundance of energy.

Taurus   In this sign, ruled by Venus and opposite to Scorpio which Mars also rules, Mars is badly placed, regardless of aspects. It is difficult for the Martian energies to express in an unblocked manner when the red planet is in this sign, and usually the blocks that are present relate to self-absorption of one kind or another. The concept of physical self-indulgence is usually present when Mars here is afflicted, as Taurus is an earth sign and sensation-oriented. The major lesson of Mars afflicted in Taurus is to *avoid self-indulgent tendencies,* especially in the sexual area.

Gemini   This sign is a mental one, ruled by Mercury, and Mars here will tend to express its energies through the mental gifts. There will be considerable mental energy present, if the positive aspects to Mars can be found. The negative aspects are concerned primarily with learning mental control, i.e. *learning to channel and direct the mental forces.* There is also a tendency for the afflicted Mars in Gemini to be mentally or verbally combative or abusive.
The strife and pugnaciousness of the afflicted Mars will, if in Gemini, tend to make the person seek out situations in which verbal spats and abusiveness will manifest.

Cancer   This sign is ruled by the Moon and is related to the concept of home, one's background, and the parental influence. In Cancer, Mars is badly placed because it is exalted in the opposite sign, Capricorn. Cancer is thus the "fall" of Mars. In Cancer, regardless of aspects, Mars will produce strife and storminess in the early home, and quite possibly in the later or adult home as well, due to the tendency to seek out a home situation in the mature life which resembles the home that one knew in childhood.
The lesson is always the same, regardless of aspect: *do not contribute to strife in the home.* Naturally the worse the aspects, the greater will be the conflicts in the home and the harder to overcome the tendency to take part in them.

Leo   This sign has its greatest problem in arrogance and pride. Mars here, when afflicted, gives a tendency to escalate arrogance into actual dislike or disdain for others. There is a tendency to have a chip on the shoulder, and to be quite antagonistic to those whose interests conflict with one's own. Often dislikes are taken to others for no apparent reason – merely that "he rubs me the wrong way".
The major lesson for Mars afflicted in Leo is to *be more accepting of* others, and to *control the feelings of antagonism.*

Virgo   Mars in Virgo, though not badly placed by the conventional tests of rulership, etc., is nonetheless in a sign that does not encourage a clear, effective expression of the energies involved. Instead, the energies tend to be frittered away in unimportant projects, excessive planning ahead, worry over health, diet and the like. The lesson – or rather the main goal – should be to *avoid wastage of energy on unworthy activities.* In positive aspect, Mars here gives strength to the mind and the ability to analyze.

Libra   Libra is the social sign – the sign that wants to be with others. It is opposite the home of Mars, namely Aries, and thus Mars here will be badly placed by sign.
Regardless of aspect, the positioning of Mars in Libra will bring about periods in the life when the person feels cut off from others, almost like an outcast. This is for karmic reasons, for it is always the case with Mars in Libra that the individual, in an earlier incarnation, has caused some other person to be shunned or driven away from society.
In the present life, the loneliness that is felt during periods of isolation is setting aside a karmic debt. In addition, Mars in Libra will bring about a tendency to create strife, argument and discord in the marriage. This is usually the fault of the person with Mars in Libra, but sometimes the partner is primarily responsible for the strife.

Scorpio   Scorpio is ruled by Mars, and the martian energies have full expression through this sign. In Scorpio, the martian energies are found mainly in the sexual area and thus the lesson is to *avoid* sexual excesses, regardless of aspect. The worse the aspects, the harder it will be to control the sexual nature. Another point that can usually be made with Mars in Scorpio afflicted is that a karmic loss must be undergone in the life — a separation from someone with whom strong sexual ties have been forged. This is, of course, to prompt the individual to place less emphasis on the sexual outlet for the energies.

Sagittarius   This sign is ruled by Jupiter, and relates to increase and bigness. In affliction, planets in Sagittarius often are related in some way to exaggeration. In the case of Mars, the tendency is to exaggerate the importance of one of the outlets for the martian energy. This could be the sexual, the athletic, the mental. Sometimes more than one of these areas is exaggerated by the individual. The more difficult the aspects, the worse the problem.

Capricorn   Mars here is dignified by being in its sign of exaltation. In Capricorn, Mars can channel the energies quite strongly into the role in life, whether this be the career, as a parent, or whatever. The danger with the afflictions to Mars in this sign is that the ability to work like a Trojan at the job or "role" will blind the individual to other aspects of life. Too much may be sacrificed due to the desire to get ahead, particularly in the personal or emotional life.

Aquarius   Mars here is in a mental or airy sign, but one ruled by the combination of Saturn (original ruler) and Uranus. In the first place, it endows the individual with considerable mental energy, regardless of aspect. In addition, it can lead to a tendency to allow the mind to play excessively with notions of sexuality, sensual fantasies, etc. This is the primary difficulty with the placement, but the strength of the mental gifts is usually such that it suffices merely to become aware of the tendency in order to bring it under control. Generally speaking, this is quite a positive placement.

Pisces   In this sign — ruled by Neptune which saps the energy and substance of everything it touches — Mars is very badly placed, regardless of aspect. There is a tendency to find that emotional "scenes" are totally exhausting, as is any necessity to deal with emotionally-polarized people. There will always be some difficulty with the feet (ruled by Pisces) and this flaw in the physical body will be for the purpose of drawing the attention down to the earth and the practical considerations. In a past life, this individual has neglected the earth-related necessities for what he considered higher pursuits and, as a result, certain souls entrusted to the care of the individual suffered in some way. Hence, it will be necessary in the present life for this individual to expend energy in a very practical way, usually in the "care and feeding" of others (children for example). Of course, numerous persons without this placement have to care for others, but in the case of Mars in Pisces, it will be more difficult and there will be some tendency to resent the fact that these responsibilities take so much of one's time and energy.

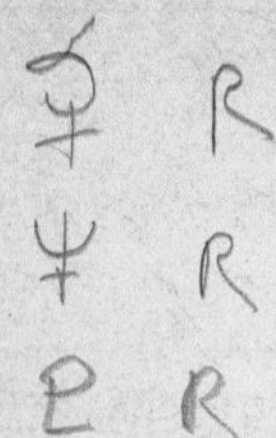

We have now dealt with the planets which act as overlays, injecting characteristics into the developing personality which would not have arisen otherwise. These planets were those relating to the triangle in man: Mercury, Venus and Mars. They are also the closest to the earth and indeed, it is for this reason that they are overlay agents. The more distant planets, beginning with Jupiter, also act in a minor way as overlays but their importance is more symbolic than causal. In other words, they have significance "by arrangement", meaning that the birth date is selected with foreknowledge of the basic pattern and plan for the life to be lived, and it is pre-arranged that the significances of the slower planets will be applicable to the life in question.

Retrograde Planets   A word is in order about retrograde planets. Much has been written lately about this phenomenon in astrological terms, and the essential concept that the energies of the planet are blocked by retrogradation has been correctly stated. However there is an underlying reason for this blockage that needs to be made clear. The limitation and obstruction is not always because of failure in a past life to learn to use the particular energy constructively (although this is often the case). In some instances, the soul has, for its own reasons, elected not to instill in the new personality the capability of expressing a particular energy represented by the planet in question. This decision is usually taken in the hope that by struggling to express the energy, the personality will learn much more fully to appreciate and to deal with the concepts and activities supported by the energy and symbolized by the retrograde planet.

Retrogradation in the planets Mercury, Venus and Mars is of no importance in causal or "overlay" terms, but it can be a signifier of blocked soul-patterns when Mercury and Venus are in conjunction with the Sun, or when Mars is in opposition to the Sun.

Jupiter

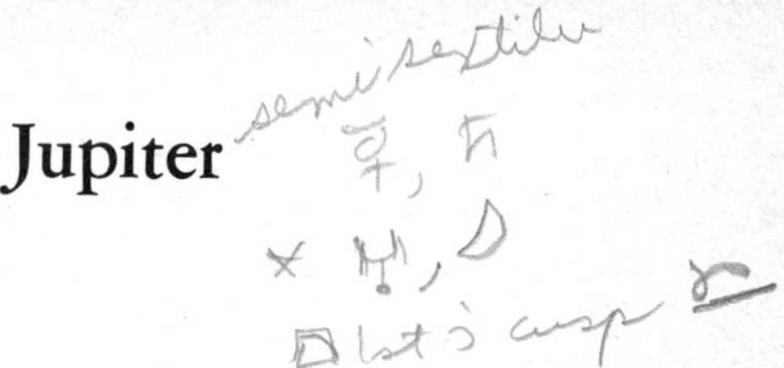

Jupiter represents the idea of bigness, increase, growth, expansion, assimilation (of food, ideas, experience, etc.), and in affliction, exaggeration. Jupiter relates to higher education, travel, religion and higher philosophical thought. It governs animals (especially the larger animals) and has much to do with the urges toward honesty, fairness and respect for the rights and freedoms of others. In the various zodiacal signs, Jupiter tells how these concepts will find expression in the life.

Aries   In Aries, ruled by Mars, Jupiter always instills a super-abundance of vital force and energy. In affliction, there can be difficulty in controlling and channelling this energy constructively. In positive aspect, Jupiter here shows good physical stamina, the ability to throw off illness, and a positive "conquering" attitude toward life. Obstacles are not much feared as there is the inner conviction that one can easily steam-roller most blockages in the life-pattern.

Taurus   In Taurus, ruled by Venus, Jupiter promises benefits of a material nature. If afflicted, there will be an over-stressing of these material benefits which will be counterbalanced by a lack in emotional, affectional fulfillment. Such a lack is meant to show the individual that material possessions are as nothing when the personal affectional life is unsatisfactory.

Gemini   In Gemini, ruled by Mercury, Jupiter brings versatility and an abundance of the mental gifts, also much travel or travel urges. Benefits come through "changing location". If such a person is ever in a rut or feels "down on his luck", he need only change residence or move to a different city in order to bring about a change for the better. In affliction, Jupiter here tends to scatter the forces, to exaggerate the importance of the mental sphere or some aspect of it, and (usually) to under-value the emotional or affectional life. Finding a balance between the mental and affectional spheres is a major task for Jupiter afflicted in Gemini.

Cancer   In Cancer, ruled by the Moon, Jupiter is in its exaltation. Inevitably with such a placement, the individual has received some definite benefit from the early home environment. This could be material, emotional, mental or just in terms of a positive self-image. In affliction, Jupiter in Cancer tends to exaggerate or over-play some aspect of one of the parents. There is often a distorted picture of one of the parental figures due to the nature of the early home experience.

Leo   In Leo, ruled by the Sun, Jupiter bestows an abundance of kindness, or at least the potential to show consideration and kindness to others. In affliction, aside from an arrogant trait, there is a tendency to exaggerate the importance of love-involvements, to enter into affairs or liasons too readily and without thought, and to allow the mind to play ceaselessly with the notion of "being in love". This is the major tendency which requires correction or moderation with Jupiter afflicted in Leo.

Regardless of the aspects to Jupiter, the Leo position always indicates that at least one of the children of the individual will do quite well in the world's eyes, will be a "success". Usually the individual will have a very close emotional tie with that child as well.

Virgo   In Virgo, ruled by Mercury, Jupiter donates the ability to write, especially short pieces, essays, stories, etc. The concentration powers are not well enough developed to tackle longer works, this problem being due to the fact that Jupiter is not well-placed in Virgo (being the ancient ruler of the opposite sign, Pisces). In affliction, these writing abilities are blocked to an extent depending upon the degree of affliction. In practical terms, the blockage is due to the mind being ceaselessly occupied with unimportant activities that waste energy: excessive planning, endless circular analysis of and going back over situations that have already happened, and so forth.

Libra   In Libra, ruled by Venus, Jupiter always promises an *eventual* happy marriage (or marriage-equivalent). The extent of the afflictions to Jupiter here suggest the degree of delay or hardship that will have to be borne first. The delays and problems are always for karmic purposes, and the ultimate happy union is also karmically deserved.

Scorpio   In Scorpio, ruled by Mars and Pluto, Jupiter promotes an excessive interest in the sensation/sexual outlet for energy. Afflicted, Jupiter here will cause the mind to play ceaselessly with the sexual fantasies and will tend to cause the individual to seek out this form of experience to an excessive degree. The major lesson is to moderate and control this tendency. In positive aspect, Jupiter in Scorpio ensures an ability to do well financially, and gives a strong sex drive.

Sagittarius   This is the home sign of Jupiter, and its ruler Jupiter here is almost wholly a positive indicator, regardless of aspect. It will denote the characteristics of honesty, candor, uprightness, a love of adventure and travel, and generally a youthful and optimistic attitude toward life.

In affliction, the youthfulness and travel urges will be exaggerated, and the candor may be emphasized to the point where the individual speaks his mind without thinking first, thus blurting out things that may hurt or offend others.

Capricorn   In Capricorn, ruled by Saturn, Jupiter is in its fall (since it is exalted in the opposite sign, Cancer). It is thus badly placed regardless of aspect. Generally, Jupiter here will indicate a suppression of the youthful, playful and adventurous instincts that most people have at least for a part of their lives. With this placement, a sober maturity is likely to be reached earlier than usual, and may sometimes be noted right from the earliest years. On the positive side, Jupiter well-aspected in Capricorn promises good success in the role in life, whether in a career, as a parent, or whatever. The worse the afflictions, the harder it will be to remain at the successful peak once attained. The key to dealing with Jupiter afflicted in Capricorn is to be prepared to shift goals as the life passes through its various phases. The early success in worldly terms must give way to progressively higher spiritual goals, or else frustration and loss will be encountered in terms of the role in life.

Aquarius   In Aquarius, ruled by Uranus, Jupiter is in a difficult placement. The energies of Uranus are not all complementary to those of Jupiter, and the usual result is that the individual feels as if the energies and abundances of his life are constantly under a threat of abrupt change or disruption. Thus the career may seem to be "hanging by a thread" or too much at the mercy of another's moods, or the marriage may be threatened regularly with currents forcing changes. All of these uncertainties are for the purpose of causing the individual to raise his sights from the material or practical level and to fix them on the distant

star of occult knowledge. This pursuit need not be in
depth — the aim is merely to get the individual to understand that hidden currents run beneath the surface of
events, that there is a plan to existence, and that success
comes easiest when one "rolls with the punches" of life,
allowing higher forces to show where the attention is next
to be directed.

In addition, Jupiter in this sign of brotherhood points to
the ability to bring together conflicting groups, to forge
closer ties between people, and to promote universal good-
will and love. The expression of this ability is the highest
calling of the person with Jupiter in Aquarius.

Pisces   In Pisces, ruled by Neptune, Jupiter is very
well placed. The emotional and feeling side of the nature is
much enhanced with this placement, regardless of aspect,
and the ability to empathize with others is pronounced. In
affliction, Jupiter here tends to exaggerate sensitivity to
the point sometimes of incapacitating the individual. The
main lesson is balance and moderation in the emotional
responses to the feelings that are picked up due to the
increased sensitivity.

Saturn

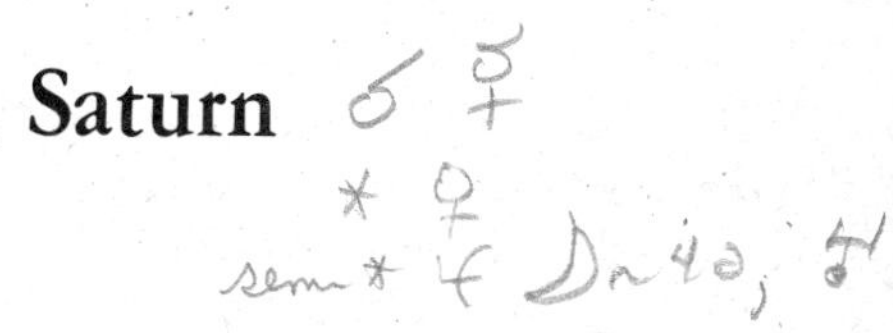

Saturn is without question the most significant <u>indicator</u> in the entire sky in terms of that which it is essential for the individual to understand about himself. In the east, it is understood that Saturn denotes karmic patterns of a life in the broad sense of the term, but western astrologers have, until recently, preferred to look on Saturn merely as an indicator of limitation, hardship and loss.

From the placement of Saturn in the birth chart can be derived the main lessons to be learned in the life, the major balancing of energies that must take place, and the extent of the negative karma that needs to be set aside. The aspects from Saturn to the other planets and the Lights tell the details of the karmic involvement of the life, and even such specifics as particular degrees of the zodiac circle have meaning where Saturn is concerned. No effort is spared by those on the higher planes in seeking to make as plain as possible to human souls in incarnation the purpose, value and goal of the lives they are living.

In specific signs, Saturn's position indicates much in terms of voluntary or imposed blockages and restrictions of a karmic nature, and Saturn's aspects to specific planets add further insight to the zodiac interpretations. In regard to the aspects of other planets, it must first be understood that each aspect acts both as an overlay in terms of the inner nature, and as a symbolic indicator coinciding with certain life patterns pre-arranged and orchestrated from the higher planes.

Aspects   When Saturn is aspecting the *Sun*, there will always be a problem within the person in dealing with one of the parental figures. The closer the aspect, the greater the problem. The same thing can be said for Saturn aspects to the *Moon*. In terms of external orchestrated events, Saturn in aspect to either of the Lights will bring into the life blockages in terms of dealing with authority, with government, with the police, or with any other authority-concept. The purpose of this pattern, both inside and out, is to bring the individual to the point of recognizing that there is value in guidelines, laws and restrictions — that man must play his "games" in accordance with rules, or else the games cannot exist. The failure to heed this lesson in past lives has led to loss and backsliding in terms of the learning of soul-lessons.

When Saturn aspects *Mercury*, there is a restriction and blockage in the free flow of mental energies into the head chakras from the higher self. The net result is to make it more difficult than usual for mental operations and manipulations to be carried out. Where Mercury is dignified by sign, however, the clamp of Saturn does not interfere seriously with the mental operations and the effect tends to be more in the outer "arranged" part of the experience. Saturn-Mercury aspects will invariably cause restraints on the Mercury-related activities: travel, schooling, communication. These will be for the purpose of prompting a fuller appreciation of these areas than was the case in a previous life, when opportunities were available but were disregarded or ignored.

When Saturn aspects *Venus*, there is inevitably an inner blockage of the flow of the heart chakra energies, resulting in emotional restriction, coldness and/or a tendency to appear unfeeling. These traits can be overcome, but only through effort. In the external life, Saturn-Venus aspects are invariably made to coincide with problems in the affectional life, separations, heartbreak, and so forth. All of these patterns, in addition to setting aside karma, have the purpose of prompting the individual to open up his own heart channels, to *feel* affection more and to show it more openly.

Saturn in aspect to *Mars* is not the terrible thing that some astrologers pretend. Mars is energy and any close Saturn aspect will tend to sit on the energies and cap them up from time to time. However, the outer circumstances of the life — even with the square or opposition — do not usually reflect the dire events that one might be led to expect from a persual of the available astrological texts. The secret here is the balancing-off of the restrictive tendency of Saturn against the expansive, not to say explosive tendency of Mars. If the individual can learn to find the mid-point between these principles, balance in the life pattern is possible. If he cannot, then wild swings between over-repressive and overly energetic states can be expected. Typically such a person finds himself under the cold, limiting hand of Saturn for extended periods, and when he cannot bear the frustration any longer, breaks free and shoots the martian energy in all directions, usually in a destructive way. This pattern is extremely broad and can be recognized in many different departments of life: love, job, health, etc. For this reason, specifics cannot be given.

Saturn aspects to *Jupiter* also pit two opposed principles against each other. Jupiter relates to increase and growing, whereas Saturn denotes contraction and restriction. Close aspects between these two will show that some of the Jupiter-ruled inner traits are repressed: youthful, adventurous urges; candor, openness and honesty; religious urges. In the outer departments of the life, there will be a similar reflection of the conflict, where *opportunities* for travel and adventure, or for higher education, are limited. The purpose both inwardly and outwardly is to prompt the individual to value more that which is restricted and witheld, because in a previous life similar opportunities were disregarded.

Saturn aspects to *Uranus* denote the conflict between that which restricts and that which wishes to break free of restriction. Therefore, whenever a close aspect of this kind occurs in a chart, the individual will find his life oscillating between periods of limitation and conformity on the one hand, and periods of unorthodox, independence-oriented experiences on the other. There will be clashes between the urges underlying these two kinds of experience, and the main lesson is to seek and find a balance between them.

Saturn aspects to *Neptune* again bring a clash into the life; this time it is between the limitation and conformity of Saturn and the escapist "dreamer" guise of Neptune. There will be a tendency to want to blur the hard outlines of daily existence by resorting to Neptunian activities, which can range from light escapist pastimes like excessive television watching to the more serious problems of drinking or drug-taking. The lesson here is obvious: to learn to accept the rigors of daily life without trying to blot out its harshness.

Saturn aspects to *Pluto* are not well understood by present-day astrologers, as these contacts are essentially in the unconscious sphere and only periodically surface into the conscious ego or into the surrounding life-pattern. The meaning of a Saturn/Pluto contact is that of an extremely far-reaching change being required in the individual in this life. It is a change that affects the unconscious sphere deeply. In some manner an attitude, outlook, way of thinking or approach to some area of the life experience must undergo a *radical* alteration, one which in almost every case will be forced upon the individual by events or circumstances *beyond his control.* The signs and houses holding the two planets will give an idea of the change that is required. Pluto will usually point to the general area, while Saturn will describe the means by which the change must come.

Saturn in aspect to the *Moon's nodes* will usually point to a major lesson to be learned in the life, this being denoted by the house and sign of the North Node. The South Node will show an area of loss or sorrow in the life, which Saturn's contact will make more serious.

In the signs of the zodiac, Saturn *always* points to a major lesson to be learned, the lesson being in some way indicated by the sign. The specifics can vary, but always the general idea can be derived from a knowledge of the sign traits and especially an understanding of the major flaws present when the *Sun* is in the sign concerned.

Aries   In Aries, Saturn denotes a lesson relating to control of the self in some way. This could mean mental, physical or emotional control.

Taurus   In Taurus, Saturn will point to a self-indulgent streak, usually of a physical kind.

Gemini   In Gemini, Saturn denotes a tendency for the mind to be too serious and weighed down.

Cancer   In Cancer, Saturn points to a problem in accepting the parent-figures that were available in the early life. Usually, the actual parents were less than satisfactory to the individual, but occasionally, the problem is entirely due to the inner traits of the individual himself. As a result of this parental problem, there is placed in the unconscious a distorted concept of what a parent should be and how a parent should act. This usually leads to activity and behavior of a negative or damaging kind when the individual himself becomes a parent. The poor parent-image in the unconscious, and the negative experiences that caused the poor image to be implanted, are karmic necessities that function to discharge the negative effects of actions taken as a parent in a previous life, which actions damaged others in some way. The major task for the person with Saturn in Cancer is to overcome the handicap arising in the early home and to evolve propler parental behaviour for himself.

Leo   In Leo, Saturn points always in the same direction: pride and arrogance. The worse the aspects to Saturn, the more grave the problem and the more pressing the need to bring about a correction.

Virgo   In Virgo, Saturn denotes a tendency to be too organized and methodical about areas that don't deserve that much energy to be expended on them. This is a placement that tends to blind the individual to the larger view of things. Details and unimportant concerns take the attention away from an appreciation of the whole. The lesson is of course to balance the lopsidedness.

Libra   In Libra, Saturn brings problems into the partnership area. Marriage is either delayed, denied or made a focus of limitation and restraint in some way. These limitations are an exterior reflection of *internal* difficulties in terms of the kind of mutual sharing that a marriage requires. This problem is always a component of the soul, and not just of the personality. The problems encountered in the marriage area are for the purpose of laying bare the internal difficulties so that the personality can attempt to rectify the internal imbalance by taking positive action to improve the partnership department of the life.

Scorpio   In Scorpio, Saturn shows always that some form of sexual problem is present in the life-pattern and must be worked on in order to be corrected. The problem is usually an over-emphasis on the sexual area, and the usual way of correcting this over-emphasis is to force the individual to endure long periods of very limited sexual expression.

Sagittarius   In Sagittarius, Saturn shows that the youthfulness and adventuresome spirit is too pronounced in the soul, and that the present life has been chosen for the correction of the imbalance. The usual means of forcing the correction is to limit travel, or to attach Saturnian characteristics to it, for example, illness or responsibilities. The individual with this placement, particularly if Saturn receives close negative aspects, should attempt to see that life calls us away to a higher adventure than merely travelling upon the physical earth. The great summons is to seek the adventures of the mind, the soaring of the spirit, and the outflowering of love for all Creation, for in these endeavors will be found the true adventure of the soul: its own progress toward the higher realms.

Capricorn   In Capricorn, Saturn is in its own sign, and is therefore very strongly placed. In general, all of the positive saturnian traits will tend to be present, and some of the negative ones depending upon the degree of affliction. The positive traits are those of seriousness, stability, caution, an instinct to seek safe positions, ambition and a strong ability to do well in the world's terms, i.e. worldly success. The negative traits are emotional coldness, an over-emphasis on worldly success, hyper-punctuality. The matter of aspects must be carefully judged as the absence of negative aspects will mean that none of the Saturn-in-Capricorn lessons are slated for the life being lived.

Aquarius   In Aquarius, which used to be ruled by Saturn before the discovery of Uranus, Saturn is also fairly well-placed. However, there is a definite tendency for this placement to coincide with an over-emphasis on the mental side of life, often to the exclusion of the emotional interchange with others. This is the greatest problem for the placement, and those especially who have Saturn afflicted here will have to undergo emotional difficulties and affectional losses in order to be brought to see the importance of developing and demonstrating affectional impulses.

Pisces   In Pisces, Saturn is very badly placed. Pisces is watery, changeable, emotional and unconcerned with practical matters. Saturn is hard, stable, extremely practical and suppressive of emotions. Thus one would expect a conflict between the different urges of these two symbols, and that is precisely what results. The individual tends to be in a tug-o'-war between hyper-emotionalism on the one hand, and the urge to be cold and rational on the other. Sometimes the conflict is between the inner traits and the kinds of experiences and people one unconsciously attracts. For example, there could be the situation where an individual with this placement is himself cold, practical, rational and reliable, but he continually finds himself dealing with emotional, unstable and impractical people. In effect, the emotionalism is also inside himself, but it is confined to the unconscious sphere and must be projected out upon others in order to be realized.

Uranus

The planet Uranus in astrology governs all that is eruptive, unexpected, unusual, occult and technically oriented. Uranus represents one of two possible responses to the limitations which Saturn imposes;
1) to break the chains, throw off the restrictions and strike out on a new path. Thus Uranus is also related to the sundering of ties and bonds, such as the marriage bond. Divorce, ruptures in love involvements and the sudden loss or departure of a loved one are all within the sphere of Uranus. Independent thought and action are included as well, and the urge to be "different".
2) to adopt a response which merely avoids looking at the restrictions and limitations, and seeks instead to blot out the harshness of reality by day-dreaming, fantasizing, or in the worst cases, turning to the oblivion that alcohol or drugs can provide. This response is quite Neptunian in nature, and Neptune will be covered more fully in the next section.

The significance of Uranus in the signs is generally not as great as that of the aspects between Uranus and the other planets, especially the "inner" planets: Sun, Moon, Mercury, Venus and Mars. Naturally those signs with obvious connections to major life-departments will provide a clear meaning for Uranus, but not all signs can be this clear. The major ones are mentioned here.
Uranus in *Taurus* (ruled by Venus) would point to changes and uncertainties in the areas of love and money, and inwardly would show that the love nature is unusual and in some way requires balancing-out.
Uranus in *Cancer*, relating to the early home, would point to unusual circumstances in the early home experience,

and usually shows that the "background" of the individual is in some way irregular or different. Inwardly, Uranus in the Moon's sign shows that, in some way, the picture or "gestalt" which the individual has of the archetypal female/mother figure is off-center or lopsided in some way. Females with this placement are often determined not to follow the model which their own mothers set, but this determination is always at odds with an even deeper wish to in fact relive the pattern which the mother laid down.

Uranus in *Leo* will naturally point to breaks, ruptures and uncertainties in the love-involvements. Inwardly this placement denotes a love nature which is unusual and lopsided in some way. The unexpected losses and sorrows in the love-involvements are intended to correct and balance the lopsidedness of the affectional nature.

Uranus in *Libra* is, of course, a pointer to changes and ruptures in the partnership/marriage department. Always this placement shows that inwardly the individual has a lopsided approach to the marriage concept. Usually it is an inability to see or appreciate the partner clearly for what he/she is.

Uranus in *Capricorn* points to changes and difficulties in the career department. Inwardly the placement denotes too great an emphasis on one aspect of the career. Typically there is too much stress on the importance of "doing well", and the sudden blockages in the career are intended to persuade the individual to ease off on this lopsided over-emphasis.

Uranus *aspects* to the inner planets will now be dealt with.

Sun   In a close aspect to the Sun, Uranus will show the inner trait of unusual interests. The negative aspects will make it harder for the individual to pursue these interests and, of course, the hindrances which present themselves are of karmic origin.

Moon Uranus in close aspect to the Moon shows the inner trait of mental agility and points to considerable ability. Negative aspects will block the channels by which this talent can be expressed, the blockage being of karmic origin.

Mercury Uranus in close aspect to Mercury shows, in positive aspect, considerable intuition and flashes of insight. The person is able to grasp ideas in an instant and does not need to work at comprehension. In negative aspects, especially the opposition, this contact disturbs the equilibrium of the mind and makes it difficult for the individual to withstand mentally stressful circumstances and situations. A risk of mental collapse or breakdown is always present with this contact, but the circumstances of the life determine whether or not such a collapse will take place.

Venus Uranus in close aspect to Venus always shows that the love-nature is in some way unusual or "different". The negative aspects point to breaks, ruptures and losses in the love-involvements, and these are always for the purpose of rectifying the imbalance in the love-nature. The positive aspects invariably point to a complex subconscious in which recollections of prior lives as a member of the other sex are as prominent as the imprint of lives in the same sex. By no means does this necessarily suggest that homosexual urges are present at the conscious level. Though this is sometimes the case, it is more usual for the confusion of sexual identity to remain at the unconscious level, and from there bring about *compensating* manifestations in the conscious life: the "super-jock", the misogynist and the mother-hater are all extreme reactions to the confusion of sexual identity which exists at the deeper levels. Much more commonly, one will find that the individual with this placement is quite choosy and hard to satisfy in terms of an appropriate partner. This stems from the subconscious awareness of the bisexual nature of the soul and a fear that this nature might bring problems in a physical relationship unless great care is taken in choosing a partner.

The way to ease the problem is, of course, to recognize *consciously* that all souls combine traits of both sexes and that individual personalities should also allow their "other side" to manifest without seeing it as a threat or a sign of "unmanliness" or "unwomanliness". Thus men may wish to expand into the artistic areas or to take an important part in child-rearing, while women can allow themselves to be more direct and foreceful with others, to seek fulfillment in a career or to express themselves more in physical and sporting activities. By thus nurturing both sides of the inner self, a balance can be struck.

Mars   Uranus in close aspect to Mars always points to a lack of self-control, usually physical self-control. The negative aspects are the most problematical in terms of angry outbursts, fits of rage and violence, but even the positive aspects call for extra effort in controlling those urges which can damage others in some way.

Neptune

The planet Neptune in astrology relates to all that is connected with the sea, water, dissolving, sapping the strength or substance of a thing, illusion, deception and escapism. In a sense, the watery film which Neptune casts over anything it touches causes difficulty in perceiving clearly the real nature of the thing. Those who have Neptune or its sign Pisces prominent in their charts will invariably find a difficulty in perceiving clearly some aspect of themselves. The sign which holds Neptune at the time of birth does not always have great significance for the individual. This is due to the slowness with which Neptune traverses the signs. In the present, all those living will have Neptune in Cancer, Leo, Virgo, Libra, Scorpio or Sagittarius. The positions in these signs will be of general importance in the sense of pointing out an area in which some form of self-deception *might* occur. However, care must be taken in determining whether the planet is strongly afflicted by aspect, for if it is not, then it is not possible to say whether the individual will definitely experience the difficulty suggested by Neptune in the particular sign.

Of greater importance is the matter of aspects to other planets. Like Uranus, Neptune tends to be more significant in its aspects to the inner planets than in its aspects to the outer ones (Jupiter, Saturn, Uranus, Pluto). The following general comments apply to aspects between Neptune and the Sun, Moon, Mercury, Venus and Mars.

Sun Neptune afflicting the Sun invariably shows a problem in clearly discerning something to do with the "male principle" within the self. Since this male principle is usually affected importantly by the relationship one has with one's father, it is often the case that that relationship was such that an incomplete picture of "male-ness" was formed in the early life due to some inadequacy or lopsidedness in the actual father.

Moon   Neptune afflicting the Moon will have an effect on the female principle in exactly the same way as Neptune/Sun affects the male principle.

Mercury   Neptune afflicting Mercury brings the whole area of communication under the confused, blurred influence of the Sea God Neptune. Usually with this placement, there is some form of problem with the speech or the ability to articulate one's thoughts. The mental processes are more obscured than usual, and some mental confusion can be present, depending upon other aspects to Mercury in the chart. This difficulty is inevitably karmic, and is applied to an individual who in previous lives failed to use mental talents fully or at all. The hope is that by having to work harder in this life to collect and channel the mental forces, the earlier disregard for mental gifts will be corrected.

Venus   Neptune afflicting Venus invariably points to considerable confusion and self-deception in regard to the affectional life. There is a tendency to "kid oneself" about love, to idealize a relationship as the "great, perfect love" — only to be disappointed when the true dimensions of the other person force themselves upon the awareness of the individual with this placement. It is essential for the person with the Neptune afflicting Venus to *see the other person clearly from the start,* in order to avoid disappointments and heartbreak.

Mars Neptune afflicting Mars is not the problem one might think in terms of the energy available. Mars is such a fount of energy that even the weakening effect of Neptune will not manage to sap its strength. But Neptune can blind the individual to the proper *use* of this energy. What is usually observed in individuals with this placement is a tendency to misuse the strength, energy or power with which they are endowed.

Pluto

The planet Pluto in astrology pertains to that which brings changes into the life — changes in attitude, changes in outlook, changes in the approach to certain areas. The changes indicated by Pluto in the chart are unavoidable and can be absolutely counted on to take place. In the case of most individuals, the changes come about "by force", i.e. they are resisted by the individual and must be rammed home by the implacable and irresistible force of events. When resistance is shown to such changes, the experiences are inevitably harder and more painful than they would have been if the individual had "seen the writing on the wall" as it were, and had voluntarily stepped in the direction in which the events were trying to move him.

The position of Pluto *by house* is by far the most important of the indicators where this planet is concerned. The houses will show the particular department of life in which the irresistible energies of Pluto will be most strongly felt. However, it is also important to note what planets, if any, are within a close orb of aspecting Pluto. Orbs less than three degrees can be taken as highly significant, and it can be concluded that the planet so aspected by Pluto is likewise pointing to an important area in which deep-rooted changes must inevitably come about in the individual.

Comments regarding Plutonian *conjunctions* are given below, since such conjunctions are always highly significant from a karmic point of view.

The conjunction to the *Sun* always shows a soul who in a past life has neglected some extremely important area of life, (marriage, children or whatever) and who must now undergo difficult experiences in the same area in order to set aside the accumulated karma. The house containing this conjunction often is a clue to the major area of neglect in the past.

The conjunction with the *Moon* is of the greatest importance as it shows an individual who has in previous lives failed to respond fully to the obligation surrounding the home or the raising of children. As a result, in the present, much in the way of heaviness and sorrow must attend the home-area in order for the karma to be offset.

The conjunction to *Mercury* is not as significant as the two already mentioned, but it too has a clear meaning. The meaning is that the mind area has in some way been neglected or *misused* in a past experience, and therefore in the present the individual must suffer in the mind in some way. The suffering may be only for a brief time, or it may last a whole lifetime, depending upon the nature of the karma involved.

The conjunction with *Venus always* shows a long period of loneliness in the life during which no affectional fulfillment can come. This is karmic for having been responsible for a similar experience undergone by another.

The conjunction with *Mars* is again not strongly significant. The meaning relates to the misuse of physical energy or the body in some way. As a result, the physical body must, in the present life, be subjected to karmic limitations, afflictions, etc., usually somewhat more severe than the usual for mankind. This is highly dependent upon other afflictions to the conjunction, however.

The Planets
in the
Houses

Introduction

The positions of the planets in the signs of the zodiac, just dealt with in Part I, are not affected by the daily rotation of the earth about its axis. With the exception of the Moon, the planets move relatively slowly from one sign to the next, the most remote ones taking years to traverse even one of the zodiacal sectors.

However, the daily rotation of the earth about its axis produces another *apparent* motion of the planets. This is best explained with reference to the Sun. Every schoolchild knows that although the Sun seems to rise at dawn, traverse the sky and then set at sundown, in reality it is the rotation of the *earth* which causes this illusion of rapid movement. In actual fact, the Sun remains relatively stationary against the fixed stars, moving only about one degree per day against the stellar backdrop. But the earth's spin, carrying us along with it as it turns, makes the sun appear to rise and set each day.

The same is true for *all* of the planets, and indeed for the fixed stars as well. As a result, it is possible to identify a planet not only by its *actual* position in the zodiac (by sign and degree), but also by its *apparent* position with respect to the viewer's location on the spinning earth. A planet may be rising on the eastern horizon, or overhead, or setting, or "down below our feet" (i.e. hidden from view by the body of the earth).

Astrologers divide into twelve sectors the path of the Sun as it *appears* to circle the earth each day. These sectors take their reference from the plane of the horizon, as seen from any given location on the earth. The Astrologer partitions the circle of the Sun's movement firstly into four quadrants: a first quadrant from the eastern horizon (the Ascendant) to the point beneath one's feet (the I.C.); a second quadrant from the I.C. to the western horizon (the Descendant); a third quadrant from the Descendant to the point above one's head (the M.C. or Midheaven); and a fourth quadrant from the Midheaven back to the Ascendant. Each of the quadrants is in turn divided into three houses, and the total of twelve houses number consecutively from the house just below the Ascendant in the first quandrant, around through the second, third and fourth quadrants, to end with the twelfth house just above the Ascendant. The diagram on the next page shows this arrangement.

The procedure for calculating the house positions of the Sun, Moon and various planets involves first determining the zodiac positions of the boundary lines dividing one house from the next. The boundary which lies at the clockwise edge of a house is called the *cusp* of that house, and is considered to be the place where the house "begins" and where its effect is the strongest. Thus, planets close to or on the cusp of a given house are taken to be more strongly influenced by that house than planets that are further "into" the house. Looking at the same figures, the cusp of the first house is the Ascendant, and the cusps of the second and third houses have been labelled. The same pattern holds for all other houses.

The conventional process for determining the house cusps employs a book called the *Table of Houses,* and requires that the astrologer know the exact *time of day* when the birth occurred (usually taken as the time of the first breath). That time is first converted to True Local Time (which compensates for the curvature of the earth), and then to Sidereal Time, using a series of mathematical steps which are beyond the scope of this book. Once the Sidereal Time of Birth has been calculated, the astrologer opens the Table of Houses at the page corresponding to the latitude of the birth location, and simply reads the house cusps for the calculated Sidereal Time.

(The foregoing procedure can be shortened and simplified considerably through the use of the Calculex Dial, which is described at the back of this book.)

There are several popular systems of house division. In one system, called "Equal House", the astrologer merely

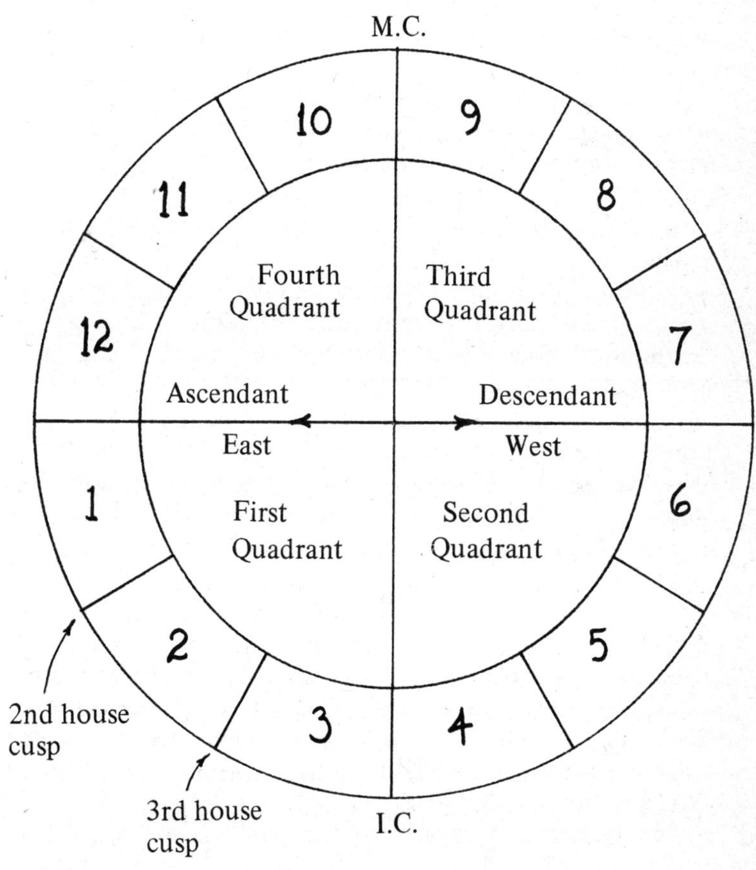

takes the Ascendant (the first house cusp) from the table of houses, then advances that point by equal increments of 30 degrees to arrive at the subsequent house cusps. For example, if the Ascendant were 14 degrees Leo, then the second house cusp would be 14 degrees Virgo, the third house cusp would be 14 degrees Libra, and so on.

Another house system — probably the most widely employed — is called the Placidus system. In this system the midheaven is used as the 10th cusp, and the quadrants are divided up according to a scheme involving rising times. There are other systems as well, and each astrologer has his favorite.

However, when I questioned Hilarion on the matter, I was told that the guides who arrange each individual's birth chart by manipulating the timing of the birth process invariably employ a system by which each quadrant is simply trisected into three equal portions, which become the three houses for that quadrant. I should point out here that, due to the earth's axial tilt, the arc spanned by each quadrant is usually different from 90 degrees. For example, the arc between the Midheaven (cusp of the 10th) and the Ascendant (cusp of the 1st), when trisected, can often yield houses which span as much as 40 degrees depending upon the time and place of the birth.

There are thus several problems confronting any non-astrologer who wishes to use the next section of this book fully to help him in self-understanding. The first is the actual time of birth to use. Many people do not know the hour and minute of their birth, and do not have any means of finding it out. Even if the time is known, one may suspect its exactness. Then there is the problem of the mathematics involved in calculating the basic Ascendant and Midheaven, and the need for a specialized reference work (Table of Houses). Finally there is the question of which house system to employ.

I wish to offer to readers of this book a way to avoid these difficulties. Hilarion is willing to provide me with an Ascendant for any person writing to request it. He points out that although this Ascendant will in many cases be the one correlating with the true first breath, in other cases it will *not* be a first breath Ascendant, but rather one yielding the best and most revealing chart for the individual in his *present* life-phase.

Using the Ascendant degree, the latitude of the birth-place and my computer, I will set up a house diagram with the house cusps filled in, and mail it out to the person making the request. All that remains to be done is to plug the planet positions into the correct houses.

I do not wish to benefit from this form of channelling, and therefore I will not make any charge for my own time. However Marcus Books must cover the cost of postage, envelopes and handling for this service, and therefore a flat cost of $2.00 must be levied for each Ascendant requested.

If you wish to have your house cusps determined in this way, please write to:

Ascendant Offer,
Marcus Books,
195 Randolph Road,
Toronto, Canada,
M4G 3S6

and include the following complete information:

1) The name and address to which the house diagram is to be forwarded.
2) For each person for whom a house diagram is required:
       - the full name
       - the birth date and year
       - the present address
       - the first breath time if known
       - the place and state/province/country of birth
       - the latitude of the birth-place
3) $2.00 for each requested diagram.

Remember that the diagram will not contain the planets. You must insert them yourself.

Prologue

The meanings to be applied to the planets when in the so-called "houses" of a birth chart differ from those signalled by the sign positions. The areas of significance for the houses are less general and more particular. Each house can be thought of as designating a "department of life" in which the events of an incarnation unfold. For example, the first house pertains specifically to the ego-picture, i.e. the self-image which the individual has developed or will develop in the present life. This self-picture can often be deeply colored with "overlays" or "filters", as indicated by the planets which the first house may hold.

It is important to understand that each of the various houses in a birth chart offers several levels of meaning — *all of which are valid and can usually be seen to be operating in the life represented by the chart.*

Essentially, a given house will have 1) a *practical* or *direct* meaning, 2) a meaning in terms of the *karma* brought over from previous incarnations, and 3) a meaning in terms of the *lessons* which the individual is intended to learn in this experience in the physical plane.

Let us give an example to illustrate these various levels. Suppose a person is born with the Moon in the first house, close to the cusp (the Ascendant). The practical effect of this placement occurs by direct influence, and can be described as a *shrinking of the self-picture,* producing feelings of inadequacy or incompetence in the individual. Such a person will tend to assume that others view him as weak or feckless and will usually be clouded with an inferiority complex of some kind. That is the immediate or practical result of this placement.

On another level, that of karmic implication, the Moon in the first house points to a need to re-balance the scales of the male-female polarity, arising from a previous life in which the male package of traits was too strongly in evidence. Often that earlier life (or series of lives) was marked by a deliberate "putting down" of women, and by an overbearing assumption of male superiority. Cruelty might also have been involved. In the present life, the karma arising from the mental, emotional or physical pain then inflicted on others must now be met and set aside — through the acute misery of self-deprecation, and the struggle to carry on despite an inner conviction of unworthiness.

The lesson aspect of the Moon in the first house will now be evident: it is to learn to temper the one-sided emphasis carried over subconsciously from that earlier male life, by cultivating some of the gentler, more retiring and compassionate traits which are traditionally associated with womankind. These meanings apply regardless of the present sex of the individual.

We are now ready to begin a discussion of the planets in the various houses.

The Sun

In the great panoply of the heavens, the Sun stands forth as far and away the most significant and most powerful factor in terms of its influence and meaning for man. Indeed, many Astrologers often forget to study the aspects of the *transiting Sun* to a birth chart when studying a natus, becoming instead engrossed in the slower moving planets. In so doing they miss one of the most significant and powerful triggers for life events. The Sun, because of its vast energy, literally influences one's circumstances through its effects on the inner attitudes of mind and emotion.

Being the dominant body in the space surrounding the earth, its effect in terms of the *practical* side of any house is simply to function as a spotlight which casts that house significance to the fore in the pattern of life events. The house which holds the Sun will be that in which much activity is observed, and around which much of the thought energy revolves. The topics which daily occupy the mind never stray far afield from the principle domain signified by the Sun's house in a natal chart. It is, in essence, *where that person lives.*

First House   Since the first house represents the ego-view or self-picture (as we have already explained), then it follows that the Sun in the first suggests that the self-image will strongly pre-occupy the mind, that the thoughts, attitudes and habits of the "native" (the person whose chart it is) will be colored by a tendency to dwell on the self and to see others and the environment as secondary in importance. "Self-absorbed" will often be an approriate adjective. Naturally, a person can learn, through persevering effort, to overcome this self-orientation of the mind (just as all negative or unbalanced traits can be corrected), but most individuals with Sun in the first find neither the inclination nor the energy to tackle a revision of that magnitude.

Another direct effect of the Sun in the first is to add a note of power to the personality. There is always a distinct aura of will and strength present in the picture that the individual projects to the world, whether or not those traits are components of the higher self. Here is an example of a direct "overlay" effect of the Sun: namely, its ability to lend a note of power and dominance to the lower self (personality) as this manifests on the earth plane. Usually such an overlay effect is deliberately added to the personality *in order to compensate for a conviction of inferiority arising from episodes in previous lives.* Thus it will often be observed that one with the Sun in the first is adept at projecting a facade of strength, will and control over the environment, while inwardly there lurks a desperate fear that others will one day discover the incompetence or the unworthiness or the self-embarassment which constantly echoes, like a mocking laugh, up from the depths of subconscious recollection.

As to the karmic implication of the Sun in the first house, this is simply stated. The main karmic significance of this placement is the necessity to pass through many testing periods in terms of the ego or self. In numerous cases a *breaking down* of the old pattern is necessary, and this may come about through a nervous crisis, through a severe depression or through manipulation by others — for example in any of a number of "cult" groups presently on the earth which practise confrontation as a technique to secure the obedience of members. This karma arises from a past life in which similar pressures were applied against others, always with a retarding influence on the soul-growth of those affected.

The lesson proposed by this solar position in a birth chart is that of integrating and "making whole" the sense of self.

It is essential to achieve balance in the multifarious facets of the personality, for without this equilibrium, little of spiritual significance can be attained. Thus, one with the Sun in the first house will typically find that he passes through numerous life-phases which seek to draw out and develop quite different traits. An intense business career may give way to a more sequestered path, or a family-oriented life-style. The man who in early life literally lives for sport and physical sensation may be drawn at a later point to the realms of mental speculation and study. The woman who thinks at first that she wants only marriage and a family, may awaken one day with a yearning for other adventures.

Second House   The second house in a birth chart represents the resources of the native. The first house is the inner resource or ego, whereas the second designates the outer means at his disposal. In the present culture such resources are usually counted in terms of money, and from this comes the traditional association of money with the second house. However, from a longer perspective this house merely governs that on the earth plane which the native can use and manipulate for his own ends.

One practical and direct significance of this solar placement relates to the necessity for the native to be careful with his resources. There is present a tendency to make rash decisions in regard to money, and due to the unwillingness to think things through beforehand, large sums are often lost. The degree of this effect depends on how afflicted the Sun is in this position.

Another direct effect is a pre-occupation with matters of the heart. Whereas the first house Sun impells the thoughts to revolve around the self or ego, the second house Sun holds the love-involvements ever before the inner perceptions of the native. There is a tendency to over-emphasize the importance of the love-relationships, which will inevitably lead to great inner suffering as links once thought permanent break asunder.

This leads to the lesson implications of the placement, which can be summed up in the simple phrase: *all for love, and the world well lost.* Here is one who would sacrifice much — even his own ego — on the altar of love. And yet, that attitude is not a true step on the path to learning love as it should be experienced — the love that Christ knew. *For the one who so avidly loves also avidly expects the love to be returned,* and it is here that the feet go astray. Pure love wishes only that the loved one be happy. It is man's *attachments and expectations* that lead him into misery, and it is only by offering these up that he attains the peace and clarity of the Saint: a deep knowing that everything of this world must fade away, and that only the life of the spirit is forever.

At the end of the long journey of suffering, man sees finally that love is not a net to ensnare, nor a lure to attract, but a beautiful, glowing lamp that lights with joy the paths of those who give it and those who receive.

The karmic implications of this placement pertain to the necessity to pass through the various episodes of emotional pain and heartbreak, because in an earlier experience others suffered likewise due to the caprice and fickleness which can yet be glimpsed in the personality of one who has Sun in the second house.

Third House   The third house of a natus (the birth chart) relates to the mental gifts of the individual. In essence, this sector of a chart shows what talents and abilities of a mental nature are at the person's disposal. The Sun in this position shows that much mental capacity is present and that the life of the mind is predominant in the hierarchy of values with which the native approaches his incarnational experience. That is the practical effect of the placement.

In lesson terms, the Sun in the third house absolutely requires the individual to pass through certain experiences which shock or force the mental conceptions into a broader framework of understanding. This often comes about through travel and the inevitable exposure to different cultures and attitudes which travel brings. For usually those with the Sun in the third house have come out of a long series of lives in which the mental conceptions were markedly narrow, bigoted or closed. And now the soul wishes to correct that earlier lopsidedness — by jostling the mind into a more universal grasp of reality.

Karmically, this placement produces the "pain of embarassment", as the narrow notions acquired by the individual in early life are seen to be juvenile or unworthy at a later point. This karma arises of course from previous lives in which others were mocked or laughed at for their views, thus embarassing them.

Fourth House   The fourth house of a birth chart has to do with the concept of "sanctuary". This portion of the diagram governs all that which provides security *in the world* for the person whose chart it is: his home, his family, his early life, his parents. The Sun in this position denotes one for whom these areas are of primary importance. Typically one of his parents will have a dominant influence on him, and this influence will produce "programs" in the subconscious which lead to problems in adulthood. There is a tendency to cling to that which has outworn its usefulness or appropriateness. The past is regarded sentimentally as having been better than the present. These effects are directly impressed on the embryonic personality at the time of birth by the closeness of the Sun to the nadir or I.C. (the cusp of the fourth house).

In karmic terms, this solar placement designates one who must pass through many episodes of insecurity in life, as the supposed mainstays of his self-confidence and contentment are chipped away at by events. He may lose his family, or home, or job, or a parent with whom he has particularly strong ties (whether of a positive or negative nature). Such a loss would have, for the person with this Sun position, a more disconcerting or devastating effect than it would if he had a different solar placement. The karma thus served arises from action in past lives when similar anxiety or trauma was caused to others.

The lesson of this solar position is simple to state: *look not to the world for security.* The only true sanctuary is the light of truth within the soul. All other lamps finally grow feeble and fail to light the way. God alone is the rock to which the discerning soul anchors his frail boat.

Fifth House   The fifth house of a Natus is that which governs the parent-child relationship. This is signified by the fact that it follows the fourth, which is a "parental" house. When the Sun is located in the fifth house, a spotlight is thrown on two areas: the native's children and the native's parents, especially the father. Indeed, it is the whole notion of fatherhood which most strongly emerges from this solar placement. The practical or direct effect of this position is to cause an increase in "distance" between the native and either his children or his father (or both if the Sun is strongly afflicted by a malefic planet). The distance may be psychological only, or it may be a *physical* separation.

The lesson of a fifth-house Sun is to de-emphasize the "love-affair" fixations and to learn to develop the two other main areas in which love should manifest: the *children* and the *parents* of the native. Indeed, many astrologers wrongly believe that the fifth house *governs* love-affairs, because malefic or disruptive planets there are observed to influence the love involvements. But it is best to take the view that the fifth-house-sun person *already* tends to over-emphasize that department of experience, and has developed a habit of *ignoring* the parent/child department. Hence, this placement, by forcing the person to be separated physically or emotionally from his children, his parent (father) or both, is prompted to learn at last to cherish *all* members of the family, regardless of generation.

Karmically, this solar position points to previous actions taken which caused anguish to his child or his parent, typically by abandoning them or "leaving them behind" in some way.

Sixth House   The sixth sector of a birth chart relates essentially to the way in which the native relates to the world, specifically the *practical, detailed* side of experience. In the sixth house, the sun points to one who has a great deal of ability to pay attention to routine, practical matters. This ability is added as a kind of "overlay" on the manifesting personality, due to the geometry of the Sun and earth at the moment of the first breath.

The lesson of this solar placement is to learn *at the higher level* the same attention to detail which the personality manifests. In almost every such case, the higher self or soul has *not* developed that trait to a sufficient degree. In past lives when the soul was unable to project that characteristic, both the native *and others* were made to suffer due to his slap-dash approach to some facet of existence, his inattention to detail, or his preoccupation with the "grander view" while neglecting the day-to-day chores and duties. Thus the gift of the Sun in the sixth is arranged so as to provide him, for this life at least, with a trait which is not fully a part of the soul. The hope is that by *practising attention to detail* throughout an entire life, the higher self will make that quality its own.

Karmically, this placement requires the person to pass through a good degree of monotonous, routine work, which the soul finds distasteful. This pattern is impressed on him because in an earlier existence he had required others to attend to similar boring and repetitive tasks, while he enjoyed the grander and more exciting occupations.

Seventh House   The seventh house of a Natus denotes the person and being of "the other". In man's philosophy, a great deal of importance has been attached to the concept of the I-other duality. Many learned tomes have been written in an attempt to come to grips with the existential questions which this duality raises. Few such philosophers, however, have perceived that there is but one resolution to the conundrums which are posed by the I-other condition: namely the idea that, in reality, *there is no I and there is no other* — for all is merely a manifestation of the One Godhead. Indeed, all aspects of the real world — every being and every thing — *are merely disguises by which God loves to surprise Himself.* For it is He alone who is the lover and the beloved, the giver and the receiver of all gifts — and the gifts too are of God.

When the sun is located in this house, there is in the personality a strong proclivity to allow the person and essence of "the other" to attain a pre-eminent place in one's value-system. The thoughts and emotions turn ever about the notions of the pair-bond, and much energy of different kinds is expended in establishing and fortifying the love-partner relationships. In practical terms, this solar placement suggests that the native must drag himself through many experiences which revolve around the notion of the "partner", even though some of those experiences may be merely inward ones.

In karmic terms, there is the necessity that much of the karma gathered in previous lives of callous or unfeeling treatment of a marriage partner must now be met. Hence the life is marked from time to time by rejection from the love partner — a rejection which is quite bitterly experienced by the native.

From the lesson point of view, this sun position calls the native to acquire a sense of *proportion* and *balance* in his attitudes toward "the other", i.e. the love partner. On the one hand, there is too strong an emphasis on the *importance* of the partner in one's life, while on the other hand there is a tendency to try to manipulate and control that other so that the native's pre-conceived ideas about how a love partnership should function will come true. Alas, the usual result of such manipulation is the very opposite of the native's desires: it is to drive a wedge of resentment between him and the partner. If he is perceptive, he will realize at last that the partner is a fully independent individual and should be cherished and honored and loved for *what he is,* rather than being coerced into conforming with the native's fantasies of what should be.

Eighth House   The eighth sector of a birth chart points to the love-interaction with "the other" — the person represented by the previous seventh house. In the present day, most such interaction has heavy sexual overtones, and this is why the eighth has come to be associated with the physical level of passion. On a deeper level, the eighth house relates to the philosophical notion of "regeneration through death", i.e. regeneration through the dying away of the old and outworn habits of thought and action. Everything which touches this house is in some way connected with the notion of "an ending and a beginning", in the sense of starting afresh after the trauma of seeing the old way expire.

When the Sun is in the eighth house, the meaning is unequivocal: *it is that the person, at some time in his life, must pass through a "dark night of the soul", from which he will emerge regenerated.* It will be a time when much of the baggage of past-life habits and reactions will be sloughed off — like a snake shedding its skin. (Indeed, the serpent is one of the symbols of Scorpio, the sign which is related to the eighth house). It often happens that, when the person is in the process of "shedding the skin", he becomes terrified that nothing will remain after that outer facade is gone. But always there is the new mode which the soul has fashioned for him — a new mode which the individual will ultimately delight to discover.

Karmically, the sun in the eighth house requires the native

to endure the "dark night", even as he had forced others to endure a similar trial in lives past.

From a lesson point of view, this solar placement beckons the individual to discover a new way of thinking and behaving, to cast himself in a new mold from which, chrysalis-like, he can emerge into a brighter day with a clearer perception of his own nature and purpose.

Ninth House   This sector of the birthchart denotes the accumulation of morality, fairness and integrity stored up from past lives. Because the positioning of many planets in this house always points to at least some lives of righteousness and honor, it can be concluded that, in the present life, a "reward" of some kind will be given. The reward is usually one which will stimulate one's higher understanding through the mind, hence the classical connection of the ninth with "higher education". But travel, too, leads to a broadening and enrichment of the mental life, and this is another "reward" arranged for one with the ninth highlighted in a chart.

The Sun in particular, when located in the ninth house, points not only to an inner character with honor and a strong sense of justice and fairness, but also to *previous* lives which likewise were marked by a ninth house emphasis, and the rewards of mental elevation and travel which this implies. Indeed, depending upon how afflicted or otherwise the Sun is found to be, the placement in question can often point to *a tendency to over-stress the higher studies and travel.* In other words, the individual has come to enjoy the "rewards for honesty" to such an extent that he now over-emphasizes them to the detriment of other factors in his life. Here we may find the person who is so engrossed in higher education or who has developed such a wanderlust, that other departments of his life remain unfulfilled. In such a case, particularly where the Sun is clearly afflicted by close squares, it can be concluded that a *deprivation* and a *limitation* must, in this life, be imposed upon his ability to explore these particular areas of earth-experience. The restriction is arranged in order to prompt him to seek more of a balanced approach to life, one in which other (usually emotional) factors are also explored and learned from.

Karmically, there is little which this solar placement implies. Hence the ninth is an exception to the general rule earlier enunciated.

From a lesson point of view, however, an afflicted Sun in the ninth sector denotes the clear requirement to *undo* the bonds of desire which tie the native to the mental and travel experiences denoted by the ninth house emphasis. When unafflicted, however, the sun in the ninth does not strongly imply any learning requirement.

Tenth House   This portion of a Natus denotes the Saturnian concepts of authority, duty and devotion. The tenth is also a parental house, and usually corresponds to that parent who was seen as having the main authority over the native when a child. Because of these general associations, and due to the fact that one's *work* in the present world-system (the Piscean) is looked on as an arena where authority, duty and responsibility must be dealt with, the tenth sector of a birth chart has come to designate the "career" in conventional astrological texts. But it is much broader than that. The tenth house really denotes the "role in life" which the person elects to play — whether that role is as a housewife, a teacher, a student, a business-person, or whatever. All of these are stage-parts which the individual acts out for the world, holds up and says "this is me" to the rest of humanity. And yet, many persons do not strongly identify with their "official roles". They have no career facade behind which they hide their real selves. Such individuals are those who have *learned the lesson of truth* — simply to be true to oneself, and not pretend to be something which inwardly one is not. This lesson is perfectly summed up in the ancient edict, "man, know thyself", and any who are truly familiar with their own inner truth will not be found among those who waste their life-energies projecting a false picture to the world.

We have digressed somewhat, but it was desired to take this opportunity to highlight what we see as one to the more deplorable tendencies found in the world today: namely the area of job/career/work. Man should not define himself in terms of what he does, but rather in terms of what he is. And when men come at last to understand the true definition of the human soul, then all of the charades and all of the pretense will melt away like butter in the sun.

For what is that true definition of man's soul? It is one known to all the great sages of the world, and it is simple to state as well: *Each individual is a child of the Love of God, and each is treasured by the Father even as an earth father treasures his own children.* No other definition strikes so clearly at the heart of the matter, for none captures so well the essence of man's relation with his God.

When the Sun is located in the tenth sector of a Natus, its meaning is that the individual has a strong drive to "project a role" into the world, to achieve something, to make his mark. This tendency is a habit built up in past lives of accomplishment.

Another practical meaning of this placement relates to the parents. Almost without exception, one with the Sun in the tenth will have come under the strong, dominating influence of one of his parents, and this relationship will have been responsible for re-kindling, in this life, the old predilection for worldly success which was assembled in past earth-experiences.

From a lesson point of view, this solar placement shows a need to learn to be true to one's own inner essence, and not to compromise that truth for the sake of success. The more afflicted is the sun, the more that lesson needs to be learned.

Karmically, the sun in the tenth sector requires the individual to pass through stages of uncertainty and worry in connection with his "role in life". The degree of affliction to the sun speaks of the seriousness of these episodes. Under great affliction, the Sun here will show one who never seems able to establish the career role he yearns for.

Eleventh House   The eleventh sector of a birth chart is largely misunderstood among astrologers at present. It is thought to govern friends and acquaintances, while in reality it is the house of *enemies*. The true house of friendship is of course the seventh, since it pertains to the one who is so close to the native that the latter is prepared to link up in some way with that person. The eleventh house, however, points to those who, in past lives, have been cast in the role of adversaries. In the present life, such former adversaries often are drawn by negative Karmic bonds into associations of one kind or another with the native, and it can happen that a friendship of a sort is struck up. However, it is wise for the individual with heavy eleventh-house influence to be mindful of the background to any of his associations which seem to be designated by eleventh-sector planets. For, knowing that such souls once were adversaries, it is possible to conduct oneself in such a way as to *overcome* the old frictions, and to bridge any lingering animosity with cords of true affection. For love alone is capable of dissolving the bonds of rivalry and dislike that tie together two souls at odds with each other. And the design of each person's eleventh house is a gift for his understanding — a signpost that can help him set his feet squarely on the path to spiritual achievement, by learning to do as Christ Himself advised when He said, "Love thine enemies".

The Sun in the eleventh house indicates that one of the parents, usually the one with the most authority over the native when a child, was once an adversary or rival in an important past life. In the present existence, it is likely that some echo of the old feelings of dislike or fear or jealousy has colored the formative years of the native, and has left him with a kind of love-hate attitude toward that parent. A further meaning is that the native will tend to form acquaintances with other authority-figures (usually older), with whom he has also had rivalrous or competitive relations in previous lives. In all such connections, it is wise to remember that here lies a golden opportunity to right past wrongs, to come to terms with a past adversary, and to learn to treat him with a genuine and heart-felt affection.

Karmically, there is a necessity with this solar placement to be exposed to a number of individuals of power and influence, who tend to take advantage of the native, and "use" him for their own ends. This is particularly so when the Sun is afflicted, and the degree of severity, as always, can be judged closely by the extent and closeness of the afflicting angles. For one with an unafflicted Sun in the eleventh, annoyances of this kind will be present but relatively minor in nature.

The lesson to be learned from this Sun position is that of loving one's former adversaries, this being an absolute prerequisite for graduation from the cycle of earth lives into which many billions of souls have trapped themselves. For hatred that is clung to and nurtured acts like a lead weight, dragging the soul again and again down into the mire of physical matter, there to meet anew the same enemy-souls that plagued his earlier experiences. The guides of such souls try always to cast them in roles that are such as to prompt a true and loving reconciliation (for example as husband and wife, or mother and child), but billions of them fail again and again. . . and their guardians weep for the chances that are lost.

Twelfth House   The twelfth sector of a birth chart is a complex and very revealing signpost in terms of the traits and characteristics which an individual brings over with him from the most recent life. We emphasize that this house points directly to the most recent life in sequence, and not to the "most important" life in terms of the present experience. As such, since much of the residue of the most recent life is stored in one's subconscious, the twelfth sector also indicates certain subconscious recollections, biases and preferences.

When the Sun is located in the twelfth, it invariably means that the individual was in the male sex in the most recent life. If the Sun is found in the early degrees of a sign (up to about 5 degrees) *and* in the twelfth, there is a strong likelihood that the immediately previous life was short compared to the average at the time. Death is likely to have occurred before age 21 was reached. This shortened experience may have had a strong impact on the individual — so much so that the present incarnation may be marked by a strong desire to live to a ripe age, or an inordinate fear of dying. Afflictions to the Sun will point to a previous life marked by adverse circumstances as signalled by the afflicting planet. For example, Saturn afflicting a twelfth house Sun suggests that the immediately previous life was marked by much responsibility and duty — and possibly illness as well. It is also likely that an illness ended that life. Afflictions from Mars to a twelfth house Sun point to a previous life marked by conflict and aggression.

From a karmic point of view, the Sun in the twelfth points to the need to pass through experiences which bring the individual into closer communication with his subconscious. He will have to undergo periods of stress and pressure which bring the contents of the subconscious mind up into the view of the conscious, observing self. In previous lives, a tendency to ignore and suppress the subconscious area has led to actions and attitudes which harmed others, hence the need now to undergo traumas which will bring a new awareness that this other vast region of the mind must be listened to.

As far as lessons are concerned, the twelfth house Sun suggests that the individual must learn to reconcile himself to promptings which arise from the subconscious. In this sense the Karmic and lesson implications of this placement are very similar.

The Moon

The house meanings have now been generally explained (in the previous chapter), and this material can be considered to apply consistently for the planets and Moon, as well as the Sun. However, each planet tell its own story different from all the rest, and as a result, the keynote ideas connected with each significating body must be blended with the basic concepts related to the house which holds that body.

The Moon is related to the ideas of nurturing and domesticity, and in particular often tells of some trait or traits which the native developed as a result of his early home experience. The people and the atmosphere which surrounded him as a child typically leave imprints on the developing personality, and these imprints can often be read in general terms by inspecting the house, sign and aspects to the moon in the Natal chart. The sign meanings have already been discussed in the first part of this book. Here we wish to deal with the significance of the various house-locations of the lunar body.

First House As already pointed out, the first house relates to the self-picture which the native has. Almost inevitably, a first-house Moon designates a *weak or inadequate self-image*. The symbolic derivation of this characteristic relies on the fact that the Moon is much "weaker" than the Sun in the sense that she shines only by reflecting the Sun's light. Hence the self-image is a mere "reflected image" symbolically speaking. Since reflected images (as in mirrors, for example) have nothing of substance to them, the self-picture of one who has the Moon in the first is likewise lacking in substance. This is to be contrasted with the first house Sun described in the previous chapter — a position which lends a great deal of strength and power to the "self" (even where such substance is not there at the higher or soul level).

The effect of the Moon in the first sector is literally to *weaken* the self-image, and this placement is often given to an individual who, in previous lives, had a strong and integrated sense of the self but who allowed the power of that strong personality to dominate and limit others. This is then the Karmic implication of Moon in the first — namely the requirement to suffer the feelings of inadequacy and unworthiness that always accompany a poor self-image, as a recompense for having put others through similar pangs in a previous incarnation.

From a lesson point of view, it is expected that the person who has the Moon in the first sector will learn to find his self-worth not in external accomplishment or the amassing of material things, but rather from the inner knowledge that he is worthy and loved in the sight of God. The antidote for the weakened self-picture which this lunar placement brings is thus to turn to the true and only source of worthiness, which is an acknowledgement of one's status as a beloved child of the Eternal Father. For in God's eyes, all creatures are noble and worthy. (see also page 90 -Ed.)

Second House   A second house placement of the Moon reveals certain important characteristics at a deep level, having to do with one's *capacity to love.* The second house is a house of affection (as well as a house designating the material resources of the native), and if it harbours the lunar body, there is a definite indication of change and fickleness in terms of the affections. The Moon is the most rapidly changing of all the bodies considered in astrology, and in the second house her fluctuating ways lend an equivalent changeability to the love-nature of the individual. The second house Moon also points to changes in terms of one's material fortunes, these being more or less traumatic depending upon aspects to the lunar body.

It often happens that one with the Moon in the second sector will not in fact perceive the variability of his affections, and will protest that he is the most constant of lovers. Alas, were it only so! In truth, here is a nature that is constant only so long as the object of the affections is out of reach. When once the desired object is attained, then the heart wanders readily to other pastures. And here is the lesson implication of a second house Moon, namely the requirement to repeatedly "fall in love" with a person who is just out of reach. These experiences are meant to teach the individual that constancy of affection which is basically lacking at the deeper level.

Karmically, the pain of almost but not quite attaining the object of one's desires is used to set aside burdens arising in earlier lives when the same inconstancy now being corrected caused equivalent pain to partners who were loved but briefly and then abandoned for other prospects.

Third House When the Moon is located in the third house in a birth chart, there is the implication that the mental activities are much stimulated, that many different areas occupy the thoughts, and that the opinions and viewpoints which the native holds are constantly in a state of flux. Here then is the major lesson area of a third house Moon, namely to avoid being like a reed blowing in the wind in terms of the opinions. Little soul-progress can be made until a person is prepared to *decide* what he believes to be true, and then to stick to that decision. In past lives, a lack of constancy in the mental sphere has typically led to an abandonment of idealism or a compromise of principles, thus deflecting the soul from the upward path. In the present life, difficulties are sure to present themselves as a result of the wishy-washy nature of the opinions and these are meant to prompt a decision to be more clear-cut in one's views, and to adhere more strongly to principles.

Karmically, the Moon in the third sector points to the

necessity of passing through periods of unsettled thought and a feeling of rudderlessness in terms of one's direction in life. In earlier incarnations, others were thrown into similar quandaries and unsettled mental states due to capricious actions taken by the individual who has a third house Moon.

Fourth House   A fourth-sector Moon is a very powerful significator astrologically, for it points to one whose natural rhythms and desires run in the direction of seclusion, isolation and the domestic routine. However, the life-pattern of this person is arranged by his guides to deny the full realization of such natural yearnings, the denial depending to a large degree on how afflicted the Moon is. The reason for the denial is to prompt the person to venture "out into the world", and to experience the demands and rewards of the rough-and-tumble existence which the earth plane offers. In a typical case, the individual with the fourth house Moon has spent too many sequestered or sheltered lives in a protective, home-like setting, and has lost his ability to fend for himself in the outside world. In many instances these sequestered incarnations have included lives in a monastery or convent — and although much can be learned and laudable soul-traits can be acquired in such secluded experiences, there is the need to balance that isolation with a period of rugged contact with the grittier side of life that most people experience in an incarnation. We have been speaking of the "lesson" side of this lunar placement.

Karmically, the picture is quite different. The individual with a fourth sector Moon has invariably placed others in positions in which they were exposed *before they were ready* to the harsher side of earth life. Often this has occurred by ejecting *children* from a protective home environment, and forcing them to confront the rough realities of the world at an early age. As a result, again depending on the degree of affliction to the fourth-sector Moon, the individual himself usually finds that he has had to undergo a similar experience at a relatively tender age. In the absence of serious affliction (especially from Saturn) the individual may escape such an episode in early life, but will still have to go through some form of (to him) undesirable exposure to the harshness of the world at a later time in his life.

Fifth House   The positioning of the Moon in the fifth sector of a birth chart has a meaning similar to that of the Sun in the same location. The only difference is that it is the concept of *motherhood* (as contrasted with fatherhood) that is being emphasized. The native must learn to accept and enjoy the role of being a mother or mother-figure (regardless of sex) and must find that closeness with his own mother and children which has been rejected in previous lives in favor of the much more "exciting" pull of the love-affair.

In order to induce the individual to scale down his emphasis on love affairs, there are arranged many fluctuations in regard to the life of the affections in terms of a partner. Love relationships will form quickly, and as quickly dissolve. Partners will come and go, and much "love activity" will be encountered — yet without the consistency and constancy of love for which the individual yearns.

Karmically, the native must be put through these ups and downs of love because his own fickleness had, in previous earth incarnations, placed others in the same kind of distress.

Sixth House   When the Moon is located in the sixth sector, the meaning is more obscure than with the houses already dealt with. The moon here points to a need to find stimulation in the *life of the mind*. The moon is one of two "mental rulers" (the other is Mercury) and as such it is not badly placed in the sixth, a sector tied to the mental sign Virgo. Yet the vibration of the sixth house and that of the Moon are not fully in harmony, since the Moon governs the lower or "everyday" mind, whereas the sixth (with its Virgo emphasis) tends more to the logical, "inventory" type of mental process. With this placement one finds a tendency to think in commonplace terms, to find the familiar within the exotic, and to blithely assume that things are simple when in fact they are complex and demanding in terms of thought.

The lesson of this placement is to recognize that there are higher mental functions than banal conversation and the planning of the day's activity. This native is called to explore the more rarefied levels of abstract thought — science, theology, the occult, mathematics, and many other subjects. At some time in his life he must come up against areas of this kind, and must learn to use his mind for more than the structuring of his everyday existence. That is the "lesson" component of the placement. Karmically, there is little that can be said that would accurately apply to all who have this lunar position.

Seventh House   Here we have a lunar placement which is extremely revealing of certain traits of the native. Specifically, this position points to one who in past lives has eschewed the company of others to such an extent that in the present experience, there is a strong tendency toward isolation and a desire to be "left alone".

Yet this trait is not one that will help weld the human family together, as the Aquarian Age requires. Therefore it is mandatory that any with the Moon in the seventh — particularly if strongly afflicted — must be thrown again and again into the company of their brothers. Only in this way can they learn to enjoy human contact. Another ploy that is used by the guides is to arrange for the native to *teach* others at different times in his life — particularly if there are strong Leo planets in the chart. In this manner the native can learn to enjoy a situation in which he must face a large number of fellow human beings and be the focus of their attention.

Indeed, it is because of a remote life in which the "focussed" attention of others led him to great pain that the native now wishes subconsciously to avoid that kind of contact. Typically it is found that a person who was hounded and persecuted by a group of people in a past life will develop an aversion to groups and a dislike for being the centre of attention. But this must be overcome, and a life with the Moon in the seventh is often chosen for the rectification of this lopsided tendency.

Another way to prompt a learning of this lesson is to promote fluctuation and change in terms of partnership (the keynote of the seventh house). Usually, a person with a seventh house Moon will find that periods of his life are marked by many ups and downs in terms of his love-partner or marriage. Often, two permanent marriage-like associations will be experienced. These fluctuations are also used Karmically to set aside burdens collected when others suffered from the native's fickle love-nature.

Eighth House   In this sector, the presence of the Moon points to an absence of the ability to *feel love*. This is not to say that such capacity is totally absent, since each human soul is able to love. But when the Moon is in the eighth at birth, it usually happens that the guides have arranged the personality in such a way that the natural channels to the higher self (soul) along which the love vibration normally flows are restricted to a greater or lesser extent (depending upon the degree of affliction to the Moon). The restriction is applied for karmic reasons *and* to teach an important lesson. The Karmic implication of this love limitation is the need to go through the "emptiness" feeling that the native once put others through by denying them love. The lesson, of course, is to struggle to allow the love feelings to manifest. With effort, the feeling of being a desert in the heart can be dissipated, and love's warm river can be prompted to flow again.

The secret to attaining this love experience is to realize that love does not depend in any way upon the sexual passions for its nourishment. In past lives, there has typically been such an emphasis on sexuality for its own sake, that the tender bloom of pure love has withered and died. This "death" is what the native is now experiencing. Love can only be revived if it is allowed to come into the heart in a *pure* way — unalloyed with the physical passions. The sexuality of man was always intended to be the *servant* of love, not its master. It was meant to be a means by which the *physical body* could express the love which was *already present in the heart*. But to allow the body sex when no love is felt is to turn the matter completely upside down. Ultimately, an over-indulgence is sex without some underlying affection between the partners will close down the channels through which the soul's love manifests in the personality. And this has generally happened to one who is born with the Moon in the eighth house.

Ninth House   The meaning of the Moon when in this sector is related to that when the Sun is here. The native is one who has accomplished much in terms of helping his brothers in past lives — especially in the nurture and care of children — and this spiritual effort results in certain "rewards" in the present life. The rewards have mainly to do with travel on bodies of water (the moon being a "watery" body, astrologically speaking), and not as much with the area of education.

Karmically, there is nothing of significance that can be said. The lesson of this placement is simply to continue to manifest the caring and nurturing habits that have become a part of the soul, without allowing the yearning for far-away places to interfere with the full development of an emotional and affectional life.

Tenth House   A tenth house Moon always points to one who is in the process of developing and rounding out a number of soul and personality facets — particularly in relation to the *talents* which the individual is able to manifest. Because (in most cases) many loose ends have yet to be "tied up", the native will normally find himself going from job to job and from career to career at relatively short intervals. These people are often concerned about the frequency of the changes affecting their role in life, but worries of this kind are unnecessary.

What is being accomplished from a lesson point of view (aside from perfecting the talents) is the realization that the self-picture and the self-worth are fully independent of any definition based on what a person does. In past lives there has been a strong tendency to identify with one's career-role, and in the present existence that habit is being dismantled through the constant change forced upon this particular department of experience.

Karmically, the placement signifies that *some* of the changes in career which the native undergoes must involve worry and uncertainty. These episodes are meant to set aside karma amassed when, in a previous life, others suffered similar mental agonies due to capricious actions taken by the native.

Eleventh House   When the Moon is located in the eleventh sector, which we have already defined as the house of (former) enemies, there is a clear indication that many of the adult *females* met with in the course of the life had once been rivals or enemies of the native (in a previous existence). This almost always applies to the native's own mother in the present life, and almost always the problem was one of rivalry for the affections of some third soul. That third soul is usually also present in the family circle — either the present father, or a sibling of the native.

The lesson of course is to overcome any residual feelings of dislike for such erstwhile enemies, especially if the mother is sensed as falling into that category.

Karmically there is the requirement to be subjected to some ill-treatment from adult female aquaintances or the mother, as recompense for having dealt out similar treatment to others.

Twelfth House   When the Moon is found in the twelfth house, it is certain that the native was a woman in the immediately previous incarnation. Knowledge of this fact alone can often provide a person with the key to self-understanding that has seemed to be missing all of one's life. If afflicted, the Moon here shows a previous life marked by sorrow and loss. If it is in an early degree and afflicted by Mars or Saturn, the Moon indicates a short life ending brutally. All of these indications are meant to provide the native with information useful to the present life, in terms of self-understanding.

From a karmic and lesson standpoint, the positioning of the Moon in the twelfth sector points to a requirement to get into closer touch with one's own subconscious. The reader is advised to read the entry for the Sun in the twelfth, since much the same approach is to be applied here.

Mercury

This planet is connected astrologically with the mind, the ability to think rationally, communication with others, and to some extent children and travel. Mercury is an asexual planet, being considered the ruler of Gemini, the twins. The twins have always been understood esoterically to be male and female twins, and Mercury as the ruler of this double sign has both male and female attributes.

Mercury speaks, then, mainly of the mental activities, talents and habits of the native. As such it constitutes an important signpost in terms of the Path on which the person has embarked in this life — for it is through the exercise of the *mind* that man rises to become a co-creator with God. We have spoken of this matter in many of our earlier writings. The reader is directed to our book, *Threshold,* for a concise explanation of the importance and proper employment of man's mental faculty.

First House   When Mercury is located in this sector of the chart, it is an indication that the view of the self is strongly colored by the notion of mental prowess. The person who has Mercury in the first, particularly if on or close to the Ascendant of the chart (the cusp of the first house) almost invariably has an *inflated* picture of his own mental abilities. The great lesson for such a person to learn is to see himself in true perspective, and especially to perceive that although he may indeed be more clever than many others, his mental qualities do not match his inflated picture of them. This will be brought home to the native repeatedly during the life experience, as he confronts fields of study with which he finds difficulty. As a result, his self-image will suffer . . . at least until he learns to scale down his exaggerated view of his own mental prowess. That is, in essence, the lesson which this placement requires the native to learn.

Karmically, there is the requirement to pass through humiliating failures in the mental realm, as a recompense for having embarassed others in a similar way in previous incarnations.

Another and rather more appealing trait normally found in those with a first sector Mercury is that of retaining a child-like, playful attitude to life, even into middle age and beyond.

Second House When Mercury is located in the second sector of a birth chart, there is a strong indication that the emotional development of the individual retains certain child-like qualities. In cases of affliction to Mercury here, there is a suggestion of immaturity in the ability to love, and this carries with it the lesson of discovering the true affectional depths of which the human spirit is capable. In order to learn this lesson, the native must be put through certain episodes of emotional pain, which will have the effect of deepening his emotional responsiveness.

Karmically, the pain in the love department is intended to set aside burdens accumulated in past lives when caprice in the affections caused others to suffer similar pain.

Third House Mercury in the third house is basically a positive placement, since the third is largely a mental house. The implication with this position is that the mental qualities are acute, and the ability to assemble factual material is present. The lesson of Mercury in the third sector is similar to one of the basic Gemini lessons, namely to avoid scattering one's forces too thinly. Karmically this placement is not significant, unless Mercury is heavily afflicted from Saturn, in which case the basic tendency toward mental depression inherent in any adverse Saturn/Mercury angle is increased.

Fourth House   Here is a position which is primarily of karmic significance. Almost invariably, the placement of Mercury in the fourth, especially when close to the cusp (the Nadir of a chart) points to a necessity for the genitals to be congenitally deficient, atrophied or malformed in some way. The degree of the problem is generally to be deduced from the closeness of afflictions to Mercury in this house. The origin of the Karmic difficulty can be varied, but usually relates to actions taken in an earlier life, by which the genital area of another person was damaged. There is little of a lesson nature in this placement.

Fifth House   In the fifth sector, Mercury tells of a person who thinks more than he ought to about love-involvements. So much mental energy is put into planning, reminiscing, hoping and imagining, that there is little *emotional* content to this department of life. In short, the native is tackling the love-involvements with his *mind* rather than with his heart, and therein lies the problem. The lesson to be learned is simply to allow the affectional life to flow on *emotional* energy, and not be so preoccupied mentally with that department. This lesson is to be mastered with the help of a situation which also is usually present with this placement: the native will interact, at some point in his life, with a *child* who will elicit great love feelings from him. The child may or may not be his own offspring. Karmically there is little significance to this placement.

Sixth House   When Mercury is in the sixth, a house vibrationally similar to Virgo (ruled by Mercury), the mental planet is basically well-placed. Mercury in this house lends to the native an analytical bent, and very often a linguistic talent. Both of these require positive aspects from slow-moving planets in order to manifest however. Karmically, there is a necessity to use that analytical mentality in work that the native finds boring or distasteful, although this requirement does not last for the whole of the life. Relief is usually given around age 45. The lesson is of course to employ the gifts of God (such as the analytical mind) in whatever work is presented, and not to complain.

Seventh House   With Mercury in the seventh sector, there is a tendency to be somewhat immature in one's approach to the marriage partner. The lesson is to "grow up" in this area, and the karmic requirements are related to earlier lives when others suffered due to that same immature approach on the part of the native. In the present life, it usually happens that at least one "important" love-bond is sundered due to the native's childish ways.

Eighth House   In the eighth house, Mercury points clearly to a sexual emphasis. This planet, as we have already said, is both male and female. In the eighth, this hermaphrodite indicator points to a deep-lying confusion in terms of the sexual roles. In a typical case, the native was in recent lives of the other sex, and had strong sexual compulsions. In the present life, now in a different sexual body, these sexual drives try to express, but produce less than complete fulfillment. The soul simply has not learned to express its sexuality in the new form, and still expects the same rewards and sensations which were known in the previous incarnations. Almost invariably, the change in sexual identity was undertaken by the soul as a means of undercutting what it saw as a drift toward indulging in sexual experience for its own sake alone, i.e. with little or no affection being felt. Since this is one of the major gateways to the downward spiral, the soul has decided to cut short that process by changing sex. Always, of course, there is a risk that the new personality, even though of different sex, may still develop a habit of sexual indulgence without love being felt; however, the likelihood of this is greatly reduced. It normally occurs that the feelings of sexual frustration felt by the new personality are interpreted by him as arising because sex for its own sake is incomplete. That is just the conclusion that the soul is hoping for, because it may impel the conscious personality to re-examine his approach to sex, and to decide that sex without love is an empty experience. Indeed, such a person will invariably find that, by allowing his sexual drives to express only with someone for whom genuine affection is felt, the feelings of frustration disappear.

Ninth House When Mercury is located in the ninth sector, there is an indication that the individual has forgotten the "precepts of righteousness" which he had acquired in earlier lives. The association of Mercury with an early childlike state is the rationale for this connection. Usually, the soul has passed from a state of "knowing" to a state of "forgetfulness" in terms of the Laws of Being, and one purpose of the present life is to restore the memory that has been eclipsed. The lesson side of this placement is thus obvious. Karmically there is a requirement that the individual pass through various episodes when his attempts to be less than completely honest and above-board will land him in hot water. This embarassment repays karma accumulated when, in a previous "righteous" life, he was so zealous in his defence of morality and probity that others were caused acute embarassment by his condemnation.

Tenth House When Mercury is located in the tenth sector of a birth chart, one finds the indicator of an individual not able to be satisfied with the "role" he is playing in the world. There is the suggestion that he is not really ready to assume full-level responsibilities in terms of working for a living. The lesson is of course to shoulder that day-to-day burden without complaint, since it "comes with the territory", i.e. is part of an incarnational experience. Karmically, the individual is forced through experiences when his inattention to detail in his job causes him problems.

Eleventh House   The location of Mercury in the eleventh is a pointer to the area where he will meet up with "those who once were enemies". Since Mercury rules children, it usually happens that the individual with an eleventh house Mercury must come to amicable terms with persons who are younger than himself. Occasionally the "former enemy" incarnates as a child of the native. The lesson is to settle the old rivalry with love. The Karma is of little importance here.

Twelfth House   When Mercury is in the twelfth sector of a Natus, the meaning is invariably that the last incarnation of the soul ended at an early age. Afflictions to Mercury will point to the circumstances of the passing in that previous existence. The analyst, knowing what happened in that recent life, will be in a better position to help the native with certain fears or phobias lodged in his subconscious patterns. The lesson relates to dealing with the subconscious baggage arising from that earlier, short life. No karmic implications exist.

Venus

Venus is the planet of love, art, beauty, affection and togetherness. Its location in a birth chart shows clearly the nature and direction of the love impulses. Under affliction, it tells of blockages to affection. In broad terms, Venus is such a positive astrological indicator that little of a karmic nature can be deduced from its placement in a natus. The lessons all revolve around learning to allow love to move freely to and from one's being, without hindrance or conditions.

First House   When Venus is in the first sector of a birth chart, there is a clear implication that the love nature of the individual is strongly tied into the self-image. The self is seen in the context of the affectional interchanges which it has with others. Under affliction, a first-house Venus can point to one whose sense of *self-worth* is too greatly dependent upon receiving love from others, and this implies the need to learn to be happy with oneself alone, not needing a constant supportive input from others.

Second House   The placement of Venus in the second house is in many ways an ideal positioning for the planet of love. The second house corresponds to the sign Taurus, which is ruled by Venus. Unless the planet is severely afflicted in the second, one may assume that the love nature of the individual is stable and genuine, and that the waters of the soul's affection run very deep. Here is one who knows that love is a constant flame. Under dire affliction, this placement of Venus can point to the need to unblock certain avenues of affection that have become

closed. Sometimes there is a tendency to lavish love on
the body, thus leading to a self-indulgent or sensuous
streak. Other than these possible problems little else need
be said.
 The placement of a benefic planet in the second sector
(Venus and Jupiter are the Lesser and Greater Benefics,
respectively) always calls into the life a protective influence over the "material resources" of the native.

Third House   When Venus is located in the third sector,
there is an indication that the mental gifts are much influenced by the course of one's affectional life. When the love
experiences run smoothly, the mental qualities function at
their best. But when heartbreak comes along, the ability to
think clearly and to use the mind productively is interfered
with. The lesson is simply to learn not to allow the vagaries
of one's emotional life to interfere with one's judgement,
rational abilities or mental qualities.

Fourth House   When Venus is located in this house, there
is present a powerful indicator that the "home base" of
the individual — the background from which he sprang or
will spring into the world — is colored by the gentle hues
of affection and love. From some source connected with
his early home, the native received a good deal of supportive love, and this has been given to him due to positive
actions undertaken in earlier lives — a kind of "earned
gift".

Fifth House   The placement of Venus in the fifth sector
points to one whose love energies tend to be directed primarily into the pair-bond or love-affair relationship, sometimes to the exclusion of other directions. Thus there will
be a preference to center the love on one's mate or partner, and to give only token affection to one's children or

parents. In order to overcome this tendency, the life pattern is usually planned so as to give to the native either as a parent or as a child, at least one soul to whom the native is extremely bound in the affectional sense. Ordinarily this will be a soul whom the native has loved as a mate in a past life. The purpose of bringing them together in a life in which they cannot again be linked in the same way is to encourage them both to explore facets of affection beyond those normally manifesting in the relationship between two mated individuals.

Sixth House   When Venus is located in the sixth house, there is a desire to surround oneself with multiple focuses of affection, although these focuses are not usually other human souls. There is an underlying wish to avoid the commitments and compromises which must be made when dealing with human beings, and therefore it often happens that the affectional impulses find expression in pets, especially cats. Cats are generally chosen because they are seen as relatively independent animals, yet cuddly enough to be loved. Dogs on the other hand tend to require more care, time and attention, and it is this giving up of one's own time and energy that the sixth-house Venus is disinclined to do. This placement carries a lesson which will be obvious in view of the foregoing explanation: namely, to learn to enter into the give-and-take of a mature, balanced affectional relation with another human soul. The life pattern is normally orchestrated in such a way as to provide this individual with at least one intense relationship in which his desire not to compromise or give of himself is severely battered away at by his yearning to be with the other person. With luck, love wins.

Seventh House   Venus in this sector represents all that is beautiful about a true mated love-relationship. Under affliction, there will be some delay in the fulfillment of the desires for an affectional partner, but that fulfillment will eventually come. The seventh house is related to the Venus-ruled sign Libra, and therefore the planet of love is very well placed in this segment of a natus. Little can be said about the lesson side of this position, aside from the need for patience and trust.

Eighth House   When Venus is located in the eighth house of a birth chart, the meaning is one which ties the love aspect of the planet into the sexual or passionate side of the eighth. It signifies that there is a danger of allowing the sexuality to determine too strongly the direction of the heart. Physical attractiveness in a potential mate may be given too great an emphasis, leading to sorrow when later the lack of emotional or mental compatibility makes itself felt. This placement carries with it the lesson of looking beyond the merely physical aspect of affection, and not being drawn into a love match solely because of the "chemistry" between the two partners.

Ninth House   When Venus is found in the ninth sector, there is a strong indication that the yearning for truth and righteousness is present in the soul. In affliction, this placement of Venus suggests that the individual needs to see the areas of integrity, honor and morality in a less emotional or extreme way. It is important to remember that all men on the earth are flawed, and that a lack of honesty is no greater a sin than a tendency toward self-indulgence, overemotionalism or egocentricity.

Tenth House   The placement of Venus in the tenth is a clear pointer to a protective influence hovering over the career/role department. At the same time there is the suggestion that the native should try to be less emotional in his daily work, particularly if Venus in this house is afflicted by squares to Mars or Saturn. The basic lesson is to achieve greater detachment when dealing with the world.

Eleventh House   When the planet of love is found in the house of former enemies, the significance is clear: that the individual sould seek ways of expressing affection for those with whom he feels an echo of the old hatred or rivalry carried over from an earlier life. If Venus is without affliction in this house, there will be given to the native at least one very deep friendship — an association that has been earned in previous incarnations by the efforts to overcome antagonisms with that same soul arising in still earlier lives.

Twelfth House   The positioning of Venus in the House governing the most recent life points to the fact that the individual was in the female sex in that life. In affliction, Venus here points to sorrow in the affections during that previous incarnation, and scars which most likely have been carried over into the present experience. Look on the Mount of Luna (the percussion) of either hand for confirmation of such subconscious scarring. It will be found as a mark, wart, sign or actual scar (refer to the Esoteric Palmistry section of our book, *Body Signs*). The lesson is to overcome any negative emotional tendencies suggested by the placement.

Mars

The planet Mars governs energy. On the positive side, it is the energy of leadership, pathfinding, and athletic endeavor. On the negative side, Mars leads to conflict, aggression and violence. The degree of affliction to Mars denotes the level of difficulty which the individual will encounter in attempting to transmute the negative martian manifestations into positive ones.

First House   When Mars is located in the first house, it is certain that the self-picture is colored by the notions of maleness, assertiveness and athleticism. If afflicted, Mars in the first will bring a strong tendency to conflict with others, to "rub them the wrong way". The lesson is simply to moderate the assertiveness and aggression to the point where the relationships with others are no longer disrupted by these traits. Karmically, this placement of Mars denotes a past life in which there was much physical aggression against others, with the result that, in the present incarnation, the individual must suffer physical abuse at the hands of others — typically one of his own parents.

Second House   When Mars is found in the second sector, there is present in the make-up a strongly passionate or physical side to the affections. Partners tend to be viewed as sexual objects first, mates second. The lesson is of course to realize that sexuality is merely the body's way of expressing love, and that such expression is always incomplete unless it has the underpinning of a strong, committed *emotional* affection. If necessary, this lesson will be learned through the loss of love partners, and such losses must continue until the individual recognizes that sex by itself is an empty experience. Karmically, this placement suggests a string of previous lives in which others suffered due to the native's sexual proclivities and the caprice that often comes with dalliance for its own sake. Thus in the current life must this individual likewise suffer, as he is attracted repeatedly to partners who are incapable of committing their affections into his care.

Third House The placement of Mars in the third house produces considerable *mental* energy, since the third is a mental house. Much ability is present to exert the mind's faculties on any problem, and when afflicted, Mars here tends to create a mind that runs on as if by its own internal process, often giving the individual sleepless nights due to the constant churning of thoughts. This condition is the result of a string of previous lives dedicated to strengthening the mental abilities. However, when such constant mental stimulus comes about in an atmosphere of pure worldliness — without the leaven of spiritual aspiration — then the present life may well have been selected by the soul as the earth-experience in which spiritual practices will have to be learned in order to be able to contend with the mind's constant turmoil.

By practising non-thinking through certain techniques available in Raja Yoga, the native can learn to still the mind, to make it smooth like the surface of a mill pond. In that quiescent state, his own intuition and the thoughts of his guides can make themselves felt. This is the main lesson of the placement. Karmically there is little that requires comment.

Fourth House When Mars is located in the fourth, there is present a clear indication that the notions of "home" and "conflict" are somehow closely bound up together. Either the early home experience or the later one (or both) are marked by conflict – usually with the native being one of the warring parties, though not always. The lesson to be learned is not to expect that all home situations are conflict-ridden, and thus not, as an adult, to erect a home environment in which antagonism and conflict reign. Usually there will be a tendency to be attracted to a partner who brings the fighting instincts out. This feistiness in the partner will be viewed as attractive, even sexually stimulating. However, such relationships are exciting only for the initial term. Soon the stimulation of the constant sparring gives way to real resentment and all-out warfare, and the relationship is in danger of foundering.

Karmically, the early-home conflict is a "meeting of self" as Cayce used to say. In previous incarnations, the native had caused his own offspring and mate much misery through his violence. Such an atmosphere always produces warpages in the psyches of children exposed to it, and it is likely that, in the present life, the native himself has been adversely affected by the conflict that marked his early home.

Fifth House   The placement of Mars in the fifth sector is extremely important, for it shows that the native has had a tendency in past lives to develop conflict-ridden relationships with either his children or his father, or both. In the present life, the same tendency will of course manifest, and the native will be cast together with souls who are again in the child or parent relation to him, and for whom he again feels resentment and anger. The lesson is to learn to overcome those distressful attitudes and feelings, for if the native does not moderate the tendency, then in a later life the same souls and the same conflict will again be encountered. And each time he fails, the task becomes harder.

If the native turns to the pair bond (love relationship) for affection while the parent/child problem remains unresolved, he will inevitably find that he cannot escape conflict, and it will surface in that relationship too. Again this is to direct him back to his primary task, which is to dismantle his feelings of dislike or resentment toward his child or his father (or both).

Sixth House   A sixth house Mars is in many ways the best placement which the planet can have. Unless severely afflicted, Mars in this sector will energize the mind, and help clarify the organizational tendencies which the individual has. When afflicted, the energies can appear somewhat skitterish and undisciplined, but all in all this position is a positive one. Many texts connect the sixth house with the health picture of the native, but in many ways this connection is misleading. There will be a multitude of exceptions to any rule connecting physical ills with sixth sector planets, even when afflicted. The best approach is to take the sixth as a mental, practical sector of the birth chart, and to assume that the planets it holds modify and explain those aspects of the individual. The connection with physical illness comes about through the fact that illnesses arise first at the spiritual or mental level, and only subsequently manifest in the physical body. Hence sixth house afflictions are pointing to mental plane imbalances and stresses which *may* manifest as physical disease, but not necessarily. It depends on how the individual deals with the disruptive energies signalled by the afflicted planets in the sixth.

Seventh House   The placement of Mars in the seventh house of a birth chart brings the disruptive energies of this planet into the life department dealing with partnerships — particularly the pair-bond partnership with a mate. Mars in the seventh sector tends to promote the selection of a mate who will allow the aggressive and disruptive tendencies of the native to be brought to the surface, where he can clearly see them for what they are, and can experience their results in terms of conflict with the mate. Generally speaking, most of his love-relationships will be marked by conflict energies.

The lesson is of course to dismantle the tendency to rush into battle when opposed, and to rise above differences on the wings of true affection. Remember that true love forgives all, and that one of the primary purposes for earth life is to learn at last that true form of compassionate affection. Karmically, the native must pass through repeated episodes in which his love-relationships founder on the shoals of conflict that he himself has created. The pain of separation is a way to discharge burdens accumulated in earlier lives when others suffered similar distress at his hands.

Eighth House   An eighth house Mars brings the sexual or passionate side of the affections strongly to the fore, and suggests that these facets of the personality are too strongly emphasized. Whether afflicted or not, Mars in this position will require the native to pass through numerous periods when sexual expression is denied him. The purpose of the denial is to prompt him to experience the other modes of affectional expression, namely the mental and emotional. If the native can learn to feel love in the heart without requiring a sexual side to its expression, then the lesson is learned. There are strong karmic implications to this placement, dealing primarily with burdens amassed during the lives when his sexual habits caused pain to others. Through enforced abstinence, these can be discharged.

Ninth House   Mars in the ninth house lends an aura of strength to the moral righteousness of the individual. He is a crusader for "justice" — whether for people, animals, nature or whatever. There is little to be learned here, except to moderate the extremes of this tendency. Karmically there is nothing that can be given which is broadly applicable to all with this placement.

Tenth House   Mars in the tenth sector gives the ability to funnel energy into the "role" in life, which normally refers to the job or career. In this sense it is comparable to Mars in Capricorn. However, in the tenth Mars also tends to bring a degree of conflict and aggression into this department. The individual must learn to soften his aggressive tendencies, otherwise his career will suffer. Positions are aften lost because co-workers are rubbed the wrong way. Karmically this placement suggests that in previous experiences on the earth plane, others were forced to undergo a loss of livelihood through the whim of the native.

Eleventh House   When Mars is located in the eleventh house of a natus, there is a clear indication that those souls who in previous lives were cast in the role of opponents or enemies will again be part of this life, and moreover that the old resentments and conflicts with such souls have yet to be resolved. A person with this martian placement would do well to survey individuals who have played "enemy" roles in his life, and to seek ways of resolving those tensions. Even if such opponent souls are no longer in contact, the individual should look within himself and find a way to dismantle any resentment or dislike which he may still be harboring. Remember that if you die to this life with the least shred of resentment or dislike for any other soul, you must inevitably be drawn back into earthly incarnation with that same soul, there again to be put through the same tensions and differences that caused the original estrangement. This law is inflexible and governs all human souls.

Twelfth House   When Mars is located in the twelfth sector, there is a clear indication that the native was in the male sex in the most recent life. Afflictions to Mars in the twelfth from the other planets speak of the general nature of that previous life, and can tell the astrological analyst much in terms of the subconscious material brought over from that existence.

Jupiter

The planet Jupiter represents the summation of "positive karma" collected in earlier lives. When Jupiter is mainly positive in its aspects from other planets (i.e. mainly trines and/or sextiles), then the benefic results of that good karma may be counted on to manifest in the present earthly incarnation. Where Jupiter is mainly afflicted (squares and/or oppostitions), then one can conclude that little positive karma can make itself felt in the present existence. We should emphasize that the "influence" of Jupiter is essentially an *arranged* one, and that the planet does not itself have any direct causal effect on individuals at their birth. By this we mean that one's guides orchestrate the events of the life to fulfill the portent which Jupiter, if well aspected, represents. Moreover, the guides ensure that, if the life is to be one in which positive karma manifests, the first breath will be taken at a time when Jupiter is well placed (or angular).

First House   Jupiter in the first house points to a secure sense of the self. However, under heavy affliction this placement denotes an *exaggeration* of the self-picture or the sense of self-importance. In such cases, the individual will estrange others because of his puffed-up attitude toward himself. His lesson is of course to learn not to project vanity or pride or vainglory — or any other manifestation of an exaggerated self-image.

Second House   Jupiter in the second sector suggests that love will be a strong part of the individual's life. If heavily afflicted however, Jupiter in the second will not give the full measure of affectional fulfillment, until the native learns to de-escalate his exaggerated view of sensual gratification.

Third House When Jupiter is located in the third sector of a natus, it is a powerful indicator that the life of the mind will be a full and pleasant experience, and particularly that the mind will be capable of greatly stretching the boundaries of its conceptions. Here is a mentality which can look with equanimity and acceptance at the most unaccustomed and strange ideas, without feeling threatened by them. This meaning applies whether or not Jupiter is mainly positive in the aspects it receives from other planets. However under heavy affliction, Jupiter in the third leads generally to a dishonest streak.

Fourth House With Jupiter in the fourth, the individual will benefit greatly from *some* positive factor in the early home. This is not to say that the early home will be beneficial in all ways, as this is rarely the case. However, Jupiter here will certainly point to at least one area which is of considerable help to the native in his later life. It could be positive reinforcement of his self-image, or wealth in the family, or an influential background, or a great deal of genuine love from at least one of the other people in the family circle. The specific nature of the benefit can often be derived from a study of the sign holding Jupiter, and the planets which most closely aspect Jupiter in a positive way. When Jupiter is heavily afflicted in the fourth, it presages a necessity to be without a "home base" during a certain part of the life.

Fifth House When Jupiter in the fifth is positively aspected, it is certain that the native will benefit from his love-involvements. Unless other planets in the fifth contradict, it is likely that the individual will have at least one child (probably several), and that one of the children will be the "apple of his eye" as the saying goes. Moreover, that child will likely become somewhat prominent when he is an adult. Under affliction, Jupiter in the fifth suggests a tendency to exaggerate the importance of love affairs generally. The afflicting planet will suggest the kind of negative result that such over-emphasis will bring.

Sixth House   If Jupiter is in the sixth and negatively aspected, the indication is that the native will receive many rebuffs in life due to his inability to interact sincerely with others. The lesson of *sincerity* is a paramount one for him, and until it is learned, little true personal happiness can be found. When positively aspected, Jupiter in the sixth suggests that the native will be happy in the daily routine of his work, and will have the capability (if he chooses to use it), of uplifting the spirits of his fellow workers.

Seventh House   Jupiter in the seventh when afflicted shows a tendency to exaggerate *some aspect* of the pair-bond or marriage relationship. The over-emphasized aspect could be *security*, or the banishment of loneliness, or the sexual gratification which a pair-bond offers. This can often be perceived by studying the nature and placement of the planets afflicting Jupiter. When well-aspected in the seventh, Jupiter promises happiness in marriage — what used to be called a "good match".

Eighth House   In affliction, Jupiter in the eighth points to a tendency to exaggerate the sexual side of love, with the attendant danger of scuttling the relationship due to the lopsided emphasis on sex. In positive aspect, an eighth-sector Jupiter points to a "windfall" experience in life. The person tends to benefit either through inheritance or through some unexpected windfall.

Ninth House   When Jupiter is located in the ninth sector of a birth chart, it points to a moral nature, one who knows what is right. Whether the person always *does* the right is another matter. That is essentially the test for anyone with a ninth house Jupiter, and many trials of this ability to choose the right action or response will be met with in the life pattern. If Jupiter is afflicted, the knowledge of the right will still be present, but the ability to adhere to honor will be weakened and the tests harder. If mainly positive in its aspects from other planets, Jupiter in the ninth indicates an honorable and upright character.

Tenth House   Jupiter in the tenth sector indicates that positive karma from past-life efforts to create something of value on the earth plane will try to manifest in this incarnation. The degree to which the manifestation comes about is judged by comparing afflictions with positive aspects in relation to Jupiter. The "manifestation of positive karma" for this placement usually results in what is perceived as "good fortune" in one's career. Even with some afflictions, Jupiter in this sector tends to be an umbrella in terms of career, allowing the person to "land on his feet", even when things seem to go against him.

Eleventh House   Jupiter in the House of Enemies, as we have renamed it, shows that much of the ancient enmity once felt for others in past lives has already been transmuted to love through effort expended in intervening incarnations. As a result, especially when Jupiter is mainly positively aspected by other planets, this life will be marked by benefit coming from influential or powerful figures — people who "take a liking" to the native because the latter tried in past lives to overcome the conflict that once had existed between them. A preponderance of negative aspects simply limits this beneficial effect.

Twelfth House   When Jupiter is located in the twelfth house of a birth chart, the indication is that the native has recently benefitted greatly from a happy and prosperous incarnation — one which he doubtless earned through efforts to benefit his brothers in still earlier lives. The result of having this happy experience on the earth plane is generally to instill a confidence that life is "all right", which can be transmitted to others in the native's circle. Afflictions to a twelfth house Jupiter tend to show what negative or limiting habits of thought might have been carried over from past lives.

Saturn

The planet Saturn is related astrologically to all that which limits and restricts man in the earth plane. It thus rules illness, authority, karma, duty and responsibility. The location of this planet in a chart always tells how at least a portion of the negative karma of the soul is to be met in this incarnation. It usually points to what the native "fears" in a subconscious sense, for the negative karma is known to the soul before birth and the personality forming on the earth plane is subliminally aware of what awaits it in the life-pattern just beginning. The house position of this planet points to the department of life where the negative karma is to be encountered.

First House   When the karmic planet is located in the house of the ego, it can be concluded that many of the traits of the self — and the self-image — are to be importantly changed through the course of this incarnation due to the pressures which Saturn's influence will bring to bear on the self-picture. The self-image must be buffeted by reverses, which will mold the character like no other influence could possibly do. The soul, prior to entering this incarnation, was vividly aware of the vast amount of work that yet needed to be done on the self-image and the basic personality which it tended to project for each physical experience, and was willing to subject that personality to a pattern of difficulty which it deemed the only salvation available. The reverses, however, may be of many kinds. In numerous cases the health is delicate — because the soul knows that much can be improved through bouts of illness. In other instances the body is strong, but accidents or operations intervene to sap its strength. In still other cases,

the physical side of the experience is left alone, and the
pressures are applied in the mental or emotional spheres
instead. Although there are no hard and fast rules to the
working out of Saturn's influence when located in the first
house, the actual nature of the reverses suffered will
always be a strong pointer to the kind of change which
needs to be effected in this life. Moreover, the faster the
native learns what the desired changes are and takes positive steps to bring them about, the faster will the pattern
of negative experience terminate. The relief of the pattern,
however, is dependent upon the extent of the negative karma to be set aside. It often happens that, even after the lesson has been learned and the requisite changes have been
made, the suffering continues. In such cases this is invariably due to the necessity to set aside more karma than has
yet been met.

Second House   When Saturn is located in the second
house, the meaning is like a sub-category of Saturn in the
first. Again there are reverses of fortune that must be
encountered, however the *department* of life in which they
will be met is more clearly delineated. It is that of the
affections. It is the love life that will most obviously be
under Saturn's hand, and this will manifest in love lost and
fulfillment delayed. We know that many with Saturn in
the second will be dismayed at this news; however we
remind the reader that earth life was not meant to be
merely an adventure in pleasure or accomplishment. Each
incarnating soul comes with many lessons and much karma, and the troubles in love are meant to allow this learning and this unburdening to take place. It is best for the
person with a second house Saturn to strive for genuineness in the affections, and for that philosophical attitude
which allows him to contemplate lost love with equanimi-

ty. It is *attachment* which brings sorrow to the human being, not the loss of a person, thing or situation. Were it not for the attachment to the thing now lost, no sadness would be felt. Indeed, when the individual has learned to love without attachment, and to love genuinely from the heart, then it is more likely that the pattern of loss will cease. It will have no other use then, even for the setting aside of negative karma.

Third House   When Saturn is located in the third sector of a Natus, the meaning has to do primarily with the mental sphere. The native will tend to be of a somewhat serious cast of mind. Where Saturn is heavily afflicted, there may be a tendency toward mental depression or instability. The details of the trait can be gathered from an inspection of the afflicting planets. If on the other hand Saturn is primarily well aspected, then the mind will tend to have a stable and perhaps even philosophical bent to it. A cautious individual, this one — especially given to planning well ahead in order to forstall any negative eventuality. The karma is largely of a mental nature, and pertains to the weight which is often felt upon the mind.

Fourth House   The placement of the ringed planet in the house pertaining to early home influences points clearly to a powerful karmic pattern involving the parental factors at work in the formation of the personality. Saturn rules authority, and the first authority with which the new personality collides is that exerted by the parents. When Saturn is afflicted in the fourth, it may be concluded that the family life was under a cloud of coldness or control, and that at least one parent represented a problem for the developing personality. Usually this problem is presented as an emotional one vis-a-vis the parent concerned and often the autocratic nature of that parent is the reason for the emotional stress felt by the native. In other cases the effect of Saturn can manifest as a *physical* distance from the parent, as contrasted with an emotional one. In some instances, at least one of the parent figures is lacking altogether.

The result of this heaviness in the early life is usually to make the individual extremely cautious when it comes to establishing his own home during adulthood. Other complexes can also be created, but these vary widely depending upon the specifics of the emotional relationship with the prominent parent signified by Saturn.

Fifth House   When Saturn is in the fifth house, it may be concluded that the relationship with the father requires a good deal of effort during that first part of the life. The native is generally one who prefers to invest his emotions in a love-relationship with a potential mate, rather than in his parental associations. This preference, carried over from a string of past lives, is now to be corrected and balanced by forcing the individual to expend effort on his relationship with his father. Even in cases where the father-figure is largely absent from the life pattern, the native must *deal* with the notion of the father. Indeed a father's *absence* is often a greater impetus to correcting one's attitude than his presence might have been.

At the same time, the placement of Saturn in the fifth house will tend to delay or deny affectional fulfillment with a mate, and to restrict the possibilities of having children. This is not to say that these areas of experience are necessarily to be denied altogether, as this only happens under severe afflictions to a fifth sector Saturn. The restrictions that are felt, however, are intended to prompt the individual to balance his expenditure of affectional energy, not placing it all into the pair-bond, but learning to distribute more to the parents (father) and to the children.

Sixth House   When the ringed planet is located in the sixth house, there is a strong indication that the working conditions for the native will be felt as restrictive and oppressive, at least over certain periods of the life. The purpose of placing him under these restrictive conditions is to inculcate a seriousness into his attitude toward his job or his role in life. He longs for an easy way to make a living, but Saturn will see to it that only through effort, perseverance and attention will he succeed.

Seventh House   The placement of Saturn in the seventh sector points to the karmic necessity for enduring a traumatic break-up of a marriage or marriage-like bond. The karma invariably stems from a life in which the native was responsible for inflicting equivalent pain on another by sundering a marriage partnership. Usually, the mate in this life is the same one who in that earlier experience suffered as the native must do now.
 However, unless Saturn receives only adverse aspects from other planets, the native will likely not be denied married fulfillment permanently. Provided he seeks earnestly the key to understanding why the marriage foundered, and strives to make the necessary changes in himself, it is likely that, at least eventually, a suitable match can be made which will be permanent.

Eighth House   Saturn in the eighth always limits sexual expression during portions of the adult life, whether through chosen abstinence, through illness of the native or his partner, or through the lack of a relationship. The purpose is always to prompt the person to de-escalate his emphasis on sexual experience. Many individuals with an eighth house Saturn may deny that they over-inflate the sexual area, but we see the matter in a different light. While in a minority of instances the native will have succeeded in dismantling his exaggeration of sex (precisely what his guides intended), in most cases the native will simply have suppressed his sexuality into the subconscious in order not to have the conscious personality tormented with desires that cannot be fulfilled (during those periods when the life-pattern enforces abstinence). In some situations, the desire of the soul to eschew sexual contact is so great (because it wants to correct earlier indulgences) that it arranges overlays and filters for the personality which will lead it to choose celibacy. Such individuals may be drawn into the church, for example, and would be incapable of understanding any hint that they harbor strong sexual urges that are now being counterbalanced.

Care must always be employed when explaining eighth-house matters to individuals, due to the ease with which those of prudish or puritanical nature can suppress their basic sexuality. However, in any case of suppression, the results can often be perceived in the health of the body (illnesses affecting the regenerative area), the dream experiences (embarassing), or markings on the forehead (creases between the eyebrows).

We caution astrologers and others in the counselling profession to use discretion when attempting to probe this area.

Ninth House When Saturn is located in the ninth house, the meaning pertains to the area of philosophy. Saturn is not at ease in the ninth, since the ringed planet is attuned essentially to worldly things whereas the ninth house is that of speculative philosophy, spiritual insight and intuition. This placement usually suggests that the individual has a tendency to develop a self-based philosophy of life, limited to that which can be objectively known and experienced. Often spiritual and "other-worldly" ideas are given short shrift as being incapable of hard demonstration. The task for the person with this Saturn placement is to broaden his perspective on life, and to develop some concept of the purpose of existence. To this end, his guides will some-

times arrange for at least one of his parents (or an equivalent) to be "into" a more spiritually-based philosophy or
religious way of life. The hope is that the native, through
exposure to this non-worldly influence, will absorb some
of the ideas which go beyond his narrow approach. If such
contact fails to jolt him out of his placid materiality, his
guides will normally begin to present him with *personal*
experiences for which his own philosophy cannot account.
These promptings will become stronger and stronger until,
unable to deny the reality of his experiences any longer, he
will turn and begin to seek a more encompassing way to
view life — one which will take these experiences into
account.

Tenth House   When Saturn is found in the tenth sector,
the meaning is that the individual must put considerable
effort into his job or career in order to make it a success.
Lacking this effort — and a good deal of care and caution
— the career will tend to turn sour again and again. The lesson is simply to devote a reasonable effort to making one's
job a success. If this is done, then no problems will be
encountered. However, past life habits of sloth and inattention have usually been brought forward into this life,
and it is these which the job reverses are meant to correct.
We should point out that the tenth house rules *any* role in
life and not merely a well-defined job or career. For a
housewife, the *home* environment is the "career" and Saturn in the tenth will have its effect there.
The tenth house is also a "parental house" and an afflicted Saturn in this position will tend to coincide with a
strained relationship with one of the parents.

Eleventh House   When the planet of karma and restriction
is located in the house of (former) enemies, the meaning is
that much effort yet needs to be expended in straightening
out the relationships with souls that once were adversaries.

The greater the afflictions to Saturn, the greater the effort that must now be made. In practical terms, this placement of Saturn will tend to bring into the life *authority figures* with whom much conflict is felt. Usually the earliest of these figures is one of the parents. If a strained and conflict-ridden relationship arises between the native and one of his parents, there is little doubt that that parent was once an enemy, and that unless the two individuals can resolve the conflict in this life, they will simply have to be tossed together again and again until the old enmity dissolves. And the only force that can do this is love.

Twelfth House   The placement of Saturn in the twelfth points to a burdened previous life, usually one marked by illness and loneliness. As a result the present personality will bear scars in the subconscious, and these residues may well program him to react to events and people in certain negative ways. The possible ramifications are too varied to allow us to comment more specifically. We will say only that this placement should be taken by the astrologer or analyst as a clue to the origins of many of the complex phobias and antisocial behaviour patterns of the native, so that other more direct methods of probing and clarification can be initiated. Past-life regression tends to be very helpful in this regard.

Uranus

Uranus is the planet of the unusual, the unexpected, the bizarre. Its energies are tapped to allow individuals — and the race as a whole — to break free of old patterns and to escape from narrowness and provincialism. The house location of this planet designates in a general way the department of life in which sudden and unexpected changes will occur. Aspects to this planet show the agency through which these changes can be expected to manifest.

First House When Uranus is located in the first sector of a birth chart, the self-image of the individual will be colored by the hues of unorthodoxy. This person dislikes the chains of convention, seeks to do things his own way, and yearns to be a free spirit. Inevitably, there will be found some particular characteristic, mark or feature connected with the physical body which sets this person apart from others. It may be the tone of voice, or an expression in the eyes, or any of a thousand possibilities. Simply look for this badge of distinction, and you shall find it.

Second House   The placement of Uranus in the second suggests an unconventional approach to affection, and sudden changes in the financial fortunes if the planet is afflicted. Especially, the native will become embroiled in at least one rather bizarre love-involvement in his life, which will leave him greatly changed.

Third House   When Uranus is located in the third sector, the meaning relates primarily to the mental sphere. It is that the mind will have the capability of grasping ideas and concepts "in a flash", without having to plod through a step-by-step reasoning process in order to understand. The specific meaning for this placement relates to the early childhood. Inevitably, a person with this Uranus position will have encountered at least one very strong adult individual whose way of thinking or behaving was quite unorthodox. That unusual individual will have exerted a powerful effect on the native during the time of their association.

Fourth House   The placement of Uranus in the fourth house points to the early home as being in some way unusual or out-of-the-ordinary. Compared to the average childhood experiences, this native will look back on a home that was marked by strong personalities, bizarre and unexpected changes, and much encouragement to "be true to oneself". Indeed, the great gift of Uranus in the fourth house lies in the circumstances of early life which give the native the courage to be different from others, to seek independence even if that entails loneliness, and to hold fast to his own views, his own convictions, his own lifestyle. In affliction, Uranus here often points to the trauma of a broken or disrupted early home.

Fifth House   When Uranus is placed in the fifth, the meaning relates to the area of love-affairs. Although the main thrust of this house is the father-child relationship, Uranus in this department tends more to point simply to an unorthodox approach to the love-involvements with the opposite sex. Inevitably, there will be at least one love-adventure which is marked by the bizarre or unusual. Either the partner will be odd, or the nature of the relationship will be of an uncommon sort.

Sixth House   A sixth house Uranus points to the propensity to rush through detailed chores requiring painstaking effort. As a result, mistakes tend to be made, and unpleasant results arise. The degree to which this manifests depends upon the relative mix of positive and negative aspects to Uranus.

Seventh House   In the seventh sector, Uranus correlates with the risk of disruption in the marriage experience. In heavy affliction, rupture or divorce becomes a distinct likelihood. This placement has karmic overtones, whereas the others already dealt with do not. The karma associated with this position of Uranus is met through the distress of marriage break-down or, in the extreme case, divorce.

Eighth House   When Uranus is located in the eighth sector of a chart, the meaning has little to do with sex. Instead it points to the financial area. Under positive aspects, Uranus here will bring "good fortune" as the positive Karma from past lives manifests. This will ordinarily be in the form of an inheritance or windfall of some sort. Under negative aspects, Uranus in this house will threaten loss through the partner's actions.

Ninth House   A ninth house Uranus offers the opportunity to expand greatly the boundaries of one's mental perceptions during the ages from 23 to 53. In that period of life, numerous individuals will be encountered who will be able to uplift and broaden the mental horizons of the native. However, the native must be willing to take the necessary steps in that direction. If he does not, then the life-pattern will close in around him, and the humdrum worries of the daily routine will seem to hem him in. The purpose of this adverse pattern is to prompt the native to open up to the next broadening influence that his guides bring his way.

Tenth House   When Uranus is located in the tenth sector, it is a clear warning to the native not to "take chances" in terms of the career or job. Speculation and "long shots" are to be avoided, if success in the world is sought. In past lives, others suffered because of the native's irresponsible attitude toward making a living, and the same trait could surface again now. To combat this, the life pattern is arranged so as to cause speculative and high-risk ventures to run into trouble. Naturally, the problem is more acute with a preponderance of negative aspects to Uranus. But even a mainly positive Uranus will require great care in the job/career area. The conventional meaning of "unusual occupation" also normally applies to this placement, and under heavy affliction to Uranus in the tenth, sudden changes in or losses of position must be expected.

Eleventh House   With Uranus in the eleventh, look to an unusual older individual to be one who, in earlier lives, was an enemy of the native. In this life there is a good chance for reconciliation between the two souls, but the oddness of the other person will tend to put the native off, to some degree. Effort and good will are needed to overcome this impediment.

Twelfth House   When Uranus is positioned in the twelfth sector of a Natus, the meaning is that the individual, in the most recent life, lived a very unusual existence. Normally, the sign holding Uranus, or the position of the planetary ruler of the sign, will give a clue to that existence. This information in the birth chart is merely meant as a first hint which will allow the astrologer or counsellor to begin to probe the subconscious contents of the native, in order to determine whether any phobias or complexes now causing problems can be traced to that earlier incarnation.

Neptune

The planet Neptune rules all that which confuses and deludes man. It also rules the sea, the oil and drug industries, and alcohol. Neptune is further associated with altered states of consciousness, mysticism, and the astral realms. The position of this watery planet in a birth chart gives a clue to the areas where the native is likely to be confused or misled, though this risk is pronounced only when the planet is under heavy affliction. If Neptune is mainly positively aspected, then its house position shows an area where some aspect of spirituality can manifest. It is difficult to give hard and fast rules to interpret the placement of Neptune in the houses, and we prefer to give only a few specific examples to demonstrate the kind of thinking that should be applied.

a) *Neptune in the First, afflicted by square to Saturn.* Here the pointer is clearly to the self-image, and the suggestion is that the native is under some strong illusion about himself. The square from Saturn suggests that this illusion was caused or influenced by the native's relation (or lack of it) to one of his parents. This pattern of meaning thus gives a possible outline which the analyst can use to probe further in an attempt to help the native overcome problems arising because of his illusions regarding himself.

b) *Neptune in the sixth well aspected by Uranus and conjunct Mercury.* Here we have an excellent pattern for the *expression* (Mercury) of spiritual or occult truth (symbolized by the positive aspect between Uranus and Neptune). Such a person could be a teacher of spiritual principles or could write about them.

c) *Neptune in the seventh conjunct Mars and well aspected by Venus.* In this case, the illusions centre around the pair-bond. Mars in conjunction must be considered an affliction to the conjoined planet, hence the risk of delusions regarding the marriage area. These delusions probably relate to conflict and aggression with respect to the mate. However the positive aspect to Venus points the way out of the problem, namely that by bringing the force of love (=Venus) into the picture, the conflicts can be overcome and the illusion (that marriage must be a battlefield) can be dispelled.

 d) *Neptune in the tenth house in opposition to the moon in the fourth, and trine the Sun.* A tenth house Neptune always suggests the risk of illusions regarding the job/career area. In this case, the Moon opposing from the fourth makes it likely that the relationship with the mother (=Moon) lies at the root of the career difficulty. The aspect from the sun also suggests a parental influence, but the positive aspect points the way to overcome the problem. That is to manifest the Sun's traits, to take positive and vigorous steps, to "shine". This advice may not seem too clear in the abstract, but any person with this planetary pattern and the associated problem will be able to perceive how it should be applied. The astrologer should simply remember the basic rules:

a) Each planet in a chart can have a *problem* associated with it;

b) Afflictions from other planets give *details* that can help *pin-point* the problem;

c) Positive aspects from yet other planets suggest ways to *overcome* or *resolve* the problem.

By using this simple rule of thumb, the astrologer can better equip himself to be of service to his brothers who suffer.

Pluto

The planet Pluto is the great bringer of change. Where this planet is located in the birth chart always designates an area or department of life in which the soul has agreed to undergo pressures promoting a deep-seated alteration in its attitudes, habits or understanding. If the personality resists these pressures, then much stress and difficulty will be felt. Pluto is like the irresistable force, sweeping all before it. The only beneficial approach to this planet's energies is to move in the direction it indicates. To do otherwise is to invite disaster.

First House   A first house Pluto tells that the individual's self-picture must be radically changed at some time during the life. The aspects which are to be got rid of can be glimpsed from a study of any planets afflicting Pluto. The "new mold" can be seen at least partly by inspecting planets which are trine to Pluto.

Second and Subsequent Houses   Basically, the approach to any Plutonian placement by house is the same as that set out in the preceding paragraph, with the areas of change being designated by the normal rulership of the house holding Pluto. The exceptions are the angular houses: fourth, seventh, tenth and twelfth (see below).

Fourth House   Pluto in the fourth, in addition to requiring deep-seated changes in the native's attitude toward the concept of the home, also indicates that one of the parents is likely to be an autocratic and coercive individual, whose will clashes repeatedly with that of the native. Yet this is a *gift* for the native, for without that clash of wills, his own pluck and determination would remain undeveloped.

Seventh House   When Pluto is in the seventh sector of a Natus, the meaning is that deep-seated changes must take place in the soul's approach to marriage. In addition, this Plutonian placement indicates a tendency to form pair-bonds with strong-willed individuals. Unless the native learns to compromise and soften his own set ways and fixed opinions, there will arise many conflicts in which both sides adopt stubborn and unyielding positions. These altercations will ultimately scuttle the marriage or pair-bond, unless the native learns the art of compromise.

Tenth House   Pluto in the tenth denotes one who tends to select a career in which deep-seated problems in his sub-conscious are to be brought to the surface and dealt with. This is in addition to the usual indication that changes in one's attitude to the role in life must take place during the incarnation.

Twelfth House   When Pluto is located in the house of the subconscious as affected by past-life experience, the meaning is basically that the most recent life was one which witnessed a number of radical changes *in the soul*. Its attitudes, habits and typical associations when incarnated likely went through a number of profound revisions. As a result, the *present* personality may be somewhat apprehensive and timid, having only recently adopted many of its present traits. Not having a long string of comparable earth personalities to back it up, the present personality will feel "out on a limb", hesitant and uncertain. The analyst can help such an individual by explaining that many *positive* changes were made in the most recent life-experience, and that the present traits of the individual represent a definite step forward in the soul's evolution.

Conclusion

Astrology, like the other primary areas of occult symbolism, has great potential in aiding individuals and the race as a whole to arrive at a higher degree of self-understanding and spiritual knowledge. Aside from this purpose, it has no valid use. Those who employ the science of the stars merely for idle fortune-telling or to achieve some form of control over others not only misuse the subject, but at the same time may acquire a heavy karmic burden — depending on what damage may have been done to others by the misuse.

We hope that, by presenting this comprehensive though somewhat simplified overview of the subject of astrology as *we* see it, those who are seeking a higher perspective from which to view themselves may find food for thought and further encouragement in their endeavors.

The best advice we can possibly give to those who wish to extend further their understanding of the subject of astrology is to meditate upon the various questions that it poses, to study all of the materials that are available on the earth plane, and lastly — whenever a particularly problematical point needs to be clarified — to *ask* the higher forces to show you the way. Remember that there is a law which governs the interchange between the earth plane and the higher levels, namely that any request for *light* (knowledge) may not be refused by a higher entity who has been asked. To refuse would mean that the higher entity would *himself* be refused in some request which *he* made to a still loftier level.

May the peace and blessing of all the higher beings who care for humanity's struggle be with you forevermore.

OM MANI PADME HUM

Glossary

Ascendant	This denotes the sign and degree rising on the eastern horizon at the time and place of birth. It is calculated by the astrologer on the basis of the date, birthplace and birth time, using a mathematical technique and a Table of Houses.
Conjunction	The occurrence of two planets (including the Sun and Moon) together in the sky, within a margin of about 8 degrees.
Detriment	The detriment of any planet is the zodiacal sign opposite the sign which the planet "rules". A planet placed in its detriment has difficulty expressing its energies smoothly.
Direct	See explanation in the Introduction.
Exaltation	The exaltation of any planet is a zodiacal sign other than its "home", in which it is well-placed and in which it can manifest its energies easily.
Fall	The fall of any planet is the zodiacal sign opposite the sign of its exaltation. A planet placed in its fall has difficulty expressing its energies easily.
"Filters"	Hilarion uses this term to designate any factors, astrological or otherwise, which may influence the development of an earth-personality, *aside* from the soul-traits which the entering individual brings with him to earth life.
Home	The home of any planet is the zodiacal sign which it primarily rules, and in which it finds the easiest and smoothest flow of its essential energies.
House	This term denotes any one of twelve divi-

sions of the space surrounding the earth. The Ascendant (q.v.) marks the beginning or "cusp" of the first house, while the Midheaven (q.v.) marks the beginning of the tenth house. Each house is thus a sector of the sky as perceived from the place and time of birth, oriented with respect to the horizon and zenith. The houses are thus distinct from the zodiac signs, which are marked out against the fixed stars.

Lights This term and the older term "luminaries" both refer to the Sun and Moon.

Midheaven This term denotes the zodiacal sign and degree which is directly overhead at the time and place of birth. Its calculation is part of the same procedure which the astrologer uses to find the Ascendant.

Moon's Nodes These are geometric points where the Moon in its trajectory crosses the earth's orbital plane. There is no actual planetary or other body at these locations.

Orb This term designates the degree of inexactitude which any aspect may have and still be considered operative. Also, it is used simply to say how far away two planets are from an exact aspect.

Retrograde See explanation in the Introduction.

Tenth House This term denotes the 30 degree sector of space eastward from the Midheaven generally above the place of birth. Planets in the tenth house are approaching the Zenith or Midheaven and are taken to have an influence on or correlation with the career area. Also, any planets in the tenth house are considered to be strongly placed *in general*, aside from their influence on the career.

Now Available

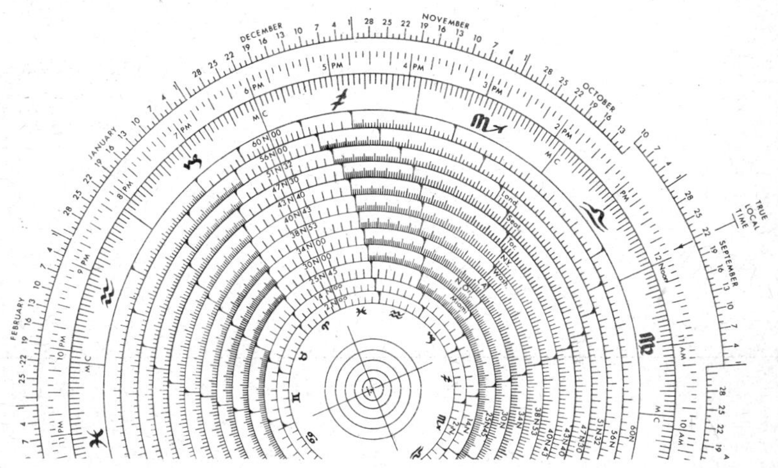

Designed by Maurice B.Cooke, the Calculex Astrological Calculator permits an instant computation of the Ascendant and Midheaven for any combination of date and birth-time. Just take two simple steps: 1) set the inner dial to the time of day; 2) set the pointer on the date. Then simply read off the Ascendant and Midheaven directly along the pointer edge. Accuracy within one degree. Manual included. (Shown above at one-half size.)

This dial, printed on sturdy cardboard with a strong plastic pointer, is especially designed to help students of Astrology who wish to avoid the tedious calculations normally required to erect a birth-chart.

To order, send a bank draft, money order or certified cheque for $8.95, payable to Marcus Books, to:

Calculex Offer,
c/o Marcus Books,
195 Randolph Road,
Toronto, Canada, M4G 3S6

(Ontario residents add $0.63 sales tax)